easy

Quicken® 2000

See it done

Do it yourself

CW00568662

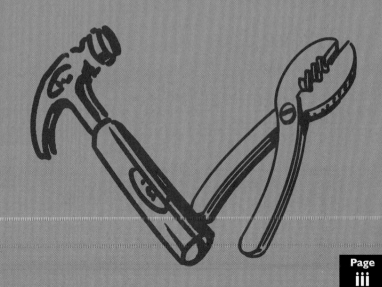

Part ▶ **6:** Using Quicken Online

Part ▶ **7:** Other Quicken Deluxe 2000 Extras

Copyright© 2000 by Que® Corporation

Printed in the United States of America

International Standard Book Number: 0-7897-2175-9

Library of Congress Catalog Card Number: 99-63711

02 01 00 99   4   3   2   1

Dedication

To my mother, Phyllis, who taught me the financial principles that have given me a firm foundation to this day.

About the Author

An author and publishing consultant, **Lisa A. Bucki** has been involved in the computer book business for more than 9 years. She wrote *PCs 6-in-1* (Que), *Easy Quicken 99* (Que), *Sams Teach Yourself Works Suite 99 in 24 Hours* (Sams), *Easy Microsoft Home Essentials 98* (Que), *Que's Guide to WordPerfect Presentations 3.0 for Windows, Managing with Microsoft Project 98* (Prima Computer Books), and *Excel 97 Power Toolkit* (Ventana). Bucki was the lead author of the *SmartSuite Millennium Edition Bible* (IDG Books Worldwide). She also has written or contributed to a number of other books and multimedia products for Macmillan. Bucki now has more than 35 author and co-author credits. Bucki has developed more than 100 computer and trade titles during her association with Macmillan. For Que Education & Training, Bucki created the Virtual Tutor CD-ROM companions for the *Essentials* series of books. Bucki recently wrote a response to a Request For Information (RFI) involving more than $300 million in business for a North Carolina–based manufacturing facility. Bucki also serves as a trainer (Word 97, Excel 97, and Project 98) for SofTrain, based in Asheville, NC.

Acknowledgments

Thank you to Angelina Ward, who invited me to make a repeat appearance as author of this Quicken book. Developer Gregory Harris and editors Leah Kirkpatrick and Victoria Elzey applied their elbow grease to ensure that this book delivers the best information to you; I hope you appreciate the results of their efforts as much as I do. Thanks, as well, to all the designers, page layout experts, proofreaders, and sales and marketing team members whose efforts ensured that this book would be on the store shelves, available for you.

Executive Editor
Greg Wiegand

Acquisitions Editor
Angelina Ward

Development Editor
Gregory Harris

Technical Editor
Jim Grey

Managing Editor
Thomas F. Hayes

Project Editor
Leah Kirkpatrick

Copy Editor
Victoria Elzey

Indexers
Aamir Burki
Christine Nelsen
Eric Schroeder

Production Designer
Lisa England

Proofreader
Jeanne Clark

Book Designer
Jean Bisesi

Cover Designers
Anne Jones
Karen Ruggles

Illustrations
Bruce Dean

How to Use This Book

It's as Easy as 1-2-3

Each part of this book is made up of a series of short, instructional lessons, designed to help you understand basic information that you need to get the most out of your computer hardware and software.

 Click: Click the left mouse button once.

 Double-click: Click the left mouse button twice in rapid succession.

 Right-click: Click the right mouse button once.

 Pointer Arrow: Highlights an item on the screen you need to point to or focus on in the step or task.

Selection: Highlights the area onscreen discussed in the step or task.

 Click & Type: Click once where indicated and begin typing to enter your text or data.

 Tips and Warnings give you a heads-up for any extra information you may need while working through the task.

2 Each task includes a series of quick, easy steps designed to guide you through the procedure.

 **Drag**

 **Drop**

How to Drag: Point to the starting place or object. Hold down the mouse button (right or left per instructions), move the mouse to the new location, then release the button.

1 Each step is fully illustrated to show you how it looks onscreen.

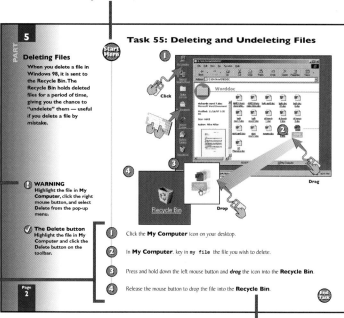

Task 55: Deleting and Undeleting Files

Deleting Files

When you delete a file in Windows 98, it is sent to the Recycle Bin. The Recycle Bin holds deleted files for a period of time, giving you the chance to "undelete" them — useful if you delete a file by mistake.

WARNING Highlight the file in My Computer, click the right mouse button, and select Delete from the pop-up menu.

The Delete button Highlight the file in My Computer and click the Delete button on the toolbar.

① Click the **My Computer** icon on your desktop.

② In **My Computer**, key in `my file` the file you wish to delete.

③ Press and hold down the left mouse button and *drag* the icon into the **Recycle Bin**.

④ Release the mouse button to drop the file into the **Recycle Bin**.

3 Items that you select or click in menus, dialog boxes, tabs, and windows are shown in **bold**. Information you type is in a `special font`. Terms found in the glossary are shown in ***bold italic***.

 Next Step: If you see this symbol, it means the task you're working on continues on the next page.

 End Task: Task is complete.

Introduction to Quicken

According to International Data Corporation, about 32 million households will be banking online by 2003. Whether you want to use Quicken to become a part of this phenomenon or you just want to better manage your checkbook, you'll soon be discovering all the benefits that Quicken Deluxe 2000 offers.

Using a computer to track your finances not only helps you organize information better but also assists you in handling financial chores like these in less time:

- Enter your bills and print checks to pay them.

- Balance your checkbook.

- Track what you spend your money on, so you can create a budget.

- Follow the progress of your investments or the declining balance on a loan.

- Download account information from your bank or pay bills online.

- Plan for tax time.

- Find financial help, investing information, and more online.

With Quicken and *Easy Quicken 2000* as your roadmap, you have everything you need to get started. You'll be spending less and saving more in no time!

Getting Started with Checking and Savings

You can use Quicken Deluxe 2000 to manage almost every aspect of your personal finances—checking, savings, investments, planning, and more. If that sounds like too much to dive into, don't worry. You can start out small and use additional Quicken features as you become comfortable and confident. This part covers fundamental Quicken tasks, so you can succeed with organizing your basic financial information.

Tasks

Creating a First Account

When you start Quicken Deluxe for the first time, the New User Setup Wizard opens and you are prompted to set up a checking account. An *account* in Quicken holds financial information for a corresponding checking (or savings or other) account at a bank or other financial institution.

✅ Register Me

If Quicken displays the Product Registration dialog box, click the **Register** button and follow the prompts to register your copy of the software. Registration offers many benefits, including free product updates you can download from the Quicken.com Web site.

✅ Your Bank

If your bank doesn't appear on the **Financial Institution** drop-down list, you can type the name of your bank in the text box.

Task 1: Completing New User Setup

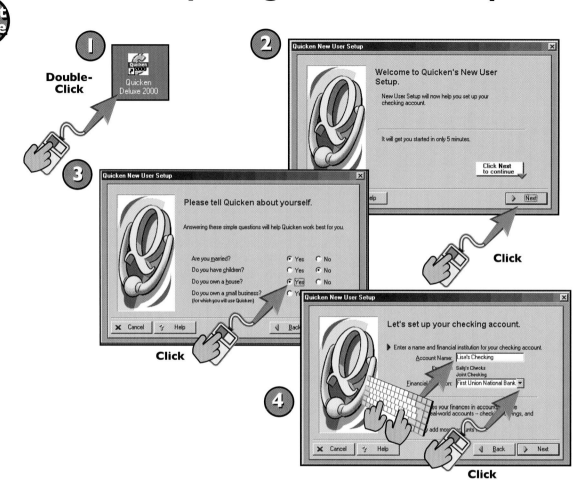

① Double-click the **Quicken Deluxe 2000** shortcut icon on the desktop.

② Click **Next** at the Quicken New User Setup welcome window.

③ Click the **Yes** or **No** option button to respond to each question about yourself, and then click **Next**.

④ Enter a name in the **Account Name** text box, choose your bank from the **Financial Institution** drop-down list, and then click **Next**.

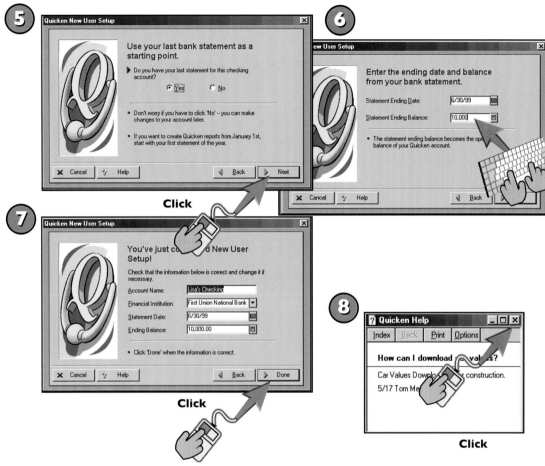

Click

Click

Click

Starting from Ground Zero

If you don't have your last bank statement and click **No** in step 5, Quicken enters 0 as the starting balance for the account. You can later change that balance by editing the Deposit column entry for the Opening Balance *transaction* in the *register* for the account. See Task 15 to learn how to make changes to a transaction in a register.

✓ **No Desktop Shortcut?**
If you don't see the Quicken Deluxe 2000 desktop shortcut icon, you also can choose **Start, Programs, Quicken, Quicken Deluxe 2000** from the Windows desktop to start the process for setting up your first Quicken account.

⑤ Get your last bank statement for the account, leave the **Yes** option button selected, and click **Next**.

⑥ Enter the **Statement Ending Date** and **Statement Ending Balance**, and then click **Next**.

⑦ Verify and correct the account information. Click **Done** to finish opening your new account.

⑧ Click the **Close (X)** button on the upper-right corner of the window to display the account register.

Task 2: Starting Quicken and Opening Your Account

Accessing Your Quicken Account

After you complete the New User Setup process to create your first account, the Quicken startup process changes slightly. On subsequent startups, Quicken presents the *My Finances Center* window, from which you can open an account or select another activity. If you choose to open an account, the register window for the account appears.

✓ Register This

An account register holds the entries for your account. The register for bank accounts (for example, checking and savings accounts) looks very similar to your paper checkbook register.

✓ Another Start

You also can choose **Start, Programs, Quicken, Quicken Deluxe 2000** from the Windows desktop to start the Quicken program.

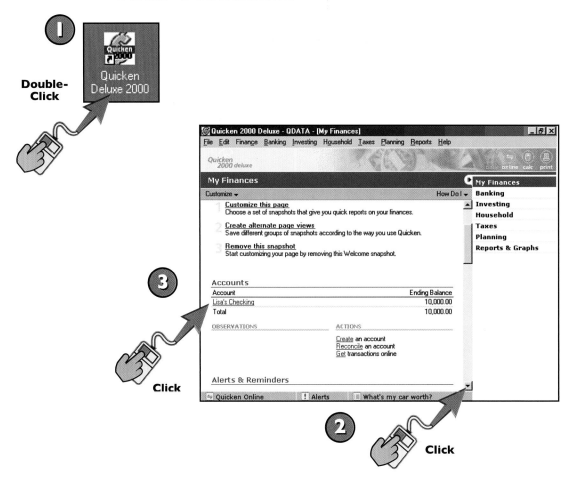

Start Here

1 **Double-Click**

3 **Click**

2 **Click**

1 Double-click the **Quicken Deluxe 2000** shortcut icon on the desktop. The My Finances Center opens.

2 Scroll down the My Finances Center until you see the Accounts List area.

3 In the **Accounts** List, click the underlined account name.

End Task

Task 3: Exiting Quicken Deluxe

Start
Here

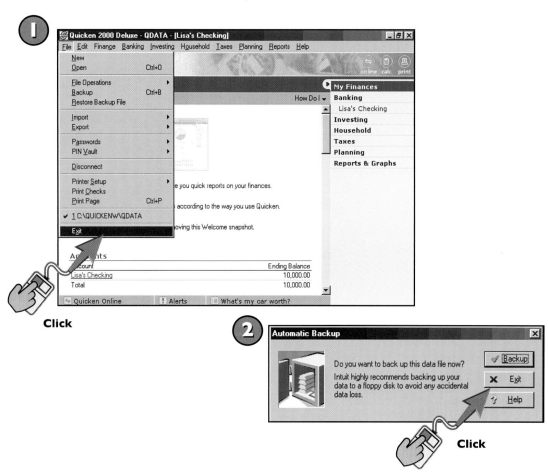

Click

Click

Finishing Your Work

When you've finished working with your Quicken account, you can close the Quicken Deluxe program and move on to other work. As you exit, Quicken Deluxe automatically saves the data file that holds your Quicken account(s), called Qdata.qdf.

✅ **To Back Up, or Not?**
When you *back up* your Quicken information, the process creates a special copy of the Qdata.qdf file. Back up your data at least once a week so you have current information to recover if the Qdata.qdf file gets damaged. To back up while exiting, click **Backup** in the Automatic Backup dialog box. Finally, follow the backup process described in Task 22 of this part.

✅ **What, No Backup?**
If you didn't make any changes to your Quicken information, you won't be prompted to back up your data when you exit.

① Choose **File**, **Exit** or press **Alt+F4**.

② If the Automatic Backup dialog box appears, click **Exit** to exit without backing up.

End
Task

Task 4: Getting Help in Quicken Deluxe

Using the Index and Contents

The Quicken Deluxe online help system offers step-by-step instructions, definitions, overview information, and other types of coverage to ensure you understand what to do. The Help Topics window offers an Index tab you can use to search for a help term, a Contents tab you can use to display help by subject, and a Find tab that you can use to search for keywords.

✓ Help at Hand

If you want help about the currently displayed window, choose **Help, Current Window,** press **F1,** or click the **How Do I** button on the window toolbar. To get help with tasks you perform in the current window, choose **Help, Troubleshooting this Window.**

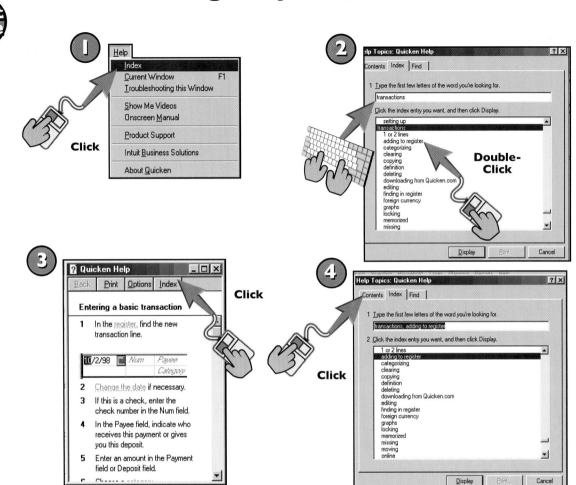

(1) Choose **Help, Index.**

(2) Type a term in the top text box and double-click the matching index entry or subentry. (If the Topics Found dialog box appears, double-click a topic.)

(3) After you review the information in the Quicken Help window, click the **Index** button to redisplay the Help Topics window.

(4) Click the **Contents** tab to display its information.

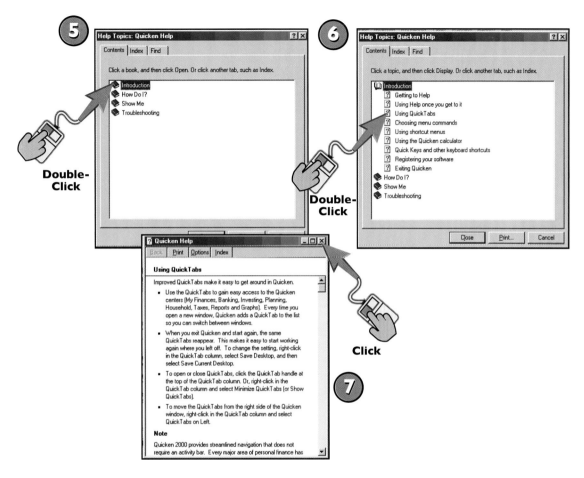

Having Quicken Show You More

To see the Onscreen Manual, choose **Help, Onscreen Manual.** Click the icon that displays the table of contents, and then click links to navigate to topics of interest. To see onscreen videos clarifying Quicken features, first insert the Quicken Deluxe CD-ROM into you CD-ROM drive. Choose **Help, Show Me Videos.** Click a topic in the list at the left side of the screen, and then press **Ctrl+R** or click the **Run** button on the video slider control to play the selected video topic.

 More About Book Icons
When you double-click some **Contents** tab book icons, the list that appears includes other book icons. Double-click one of these icons to open it and double-click the icon again to close it.

⑤ Double-click a book icon to open it and display a list of topics.

⑥ Double-click a page icon to see help about that topic.

⑦ After you finish reviewing the help information, click the **Close** button on the Quicken Help window to exit Help.

Task 5: Navigating in Quicken Deluxe

Using Quicken's Screen Features

In addition to the My Finances Center, Quicken Deluxe 2000 gives you six Financial Activity Centers, listed in the *QuickTab* column at the right side of the screen. You can click a QuickTab to display the specified center. For each account you add or activity you open within a center, Quicken adds another QuickTab, each of which represents a separate window. You can use a QuickTab to move quickly to another window or center, or you can hide the QuickTab column to have more working area onscreen.

✓ **Missing QuickTabs**
The screen examples in this book may not show QuickTabs in all instances, because of the space they take up onscreen.

Start Here

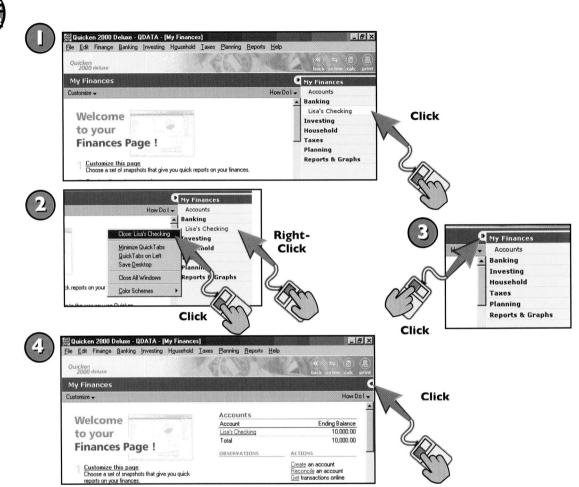

1. Click a **QuickTab** to display its window or center, making that window or center active.

2. To close a window, right-click its **QuickTab** and click the **Close: (Window Name)** command at the top of the shortcut menu.

3. To hide (minimize) the QuickTab column, click the handle for the column.

4. To redisplay the QuickTab column, click the handle again.

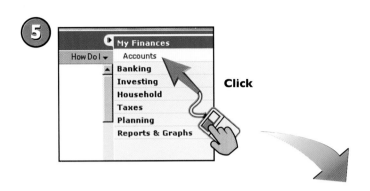

Click

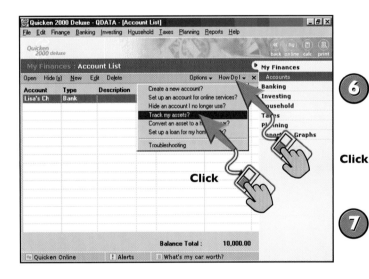

Click

Click

Click

Finding Commands and Activities

The Quicken Deluxe window includes a menu bar at the top of the screen. The menu bar organizes commands in menus. The toolbar at the top of a specific active window, such as an account window, lists a number of buttons. When you click a plain button, Quicken performs the command or displays a dialog box. Clicking a button with a triangle in its name displays a menu of commands.

⑤ Click a window's QuickTab to display that window.

⑥ Click a toolbar button with a triangle to open a menu of commands.

⑦ Click the command you want, and then complete any dialog boxes, if needed.

✅ Open Centers
You can click the **Close (X)** button at the right end of a window toolbar to close a window. You can't, however, close a Financial Activity Center.

✅ Status Bar Alerts
Click a button on the Quicken status bar to set it up to display various alerts or to access selected features.

End Task

Task 6: Adding Another Bank Account

Matching Your Real-World Accounts

Your bank or financial institution divides your money into different accounts with different features. You might have multiple accounts, perhaps at different banks. To accurately track your account information in Quicken, you need to set up a Quicken bank account to hold the entries (transactions) for each of your real-world accounts. The process is virtually the same for all bank accounts.

ⓘ WARNING

Quicken Deluxe adds all new accounts you create to the QDATA file, a Quicken data file. If you want to keep another person's financial information completely separate from yours, create another account file, as described in Part 7, Task 1. Then add that person's new accounts to the new file.

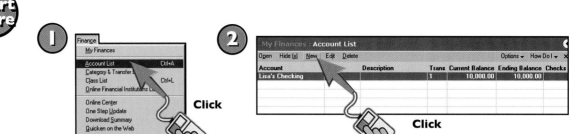

(1) Choose **Finance**, **Account List** (**Ctrl+A**) to display the Account List.

(2) Click the **New** button.

(3) Click the option button for the type of account to create, and then click **Next**.

(4) Enter an **Account Name** and **Description**, enter or select a **Financial Institution**, and click **Next**.

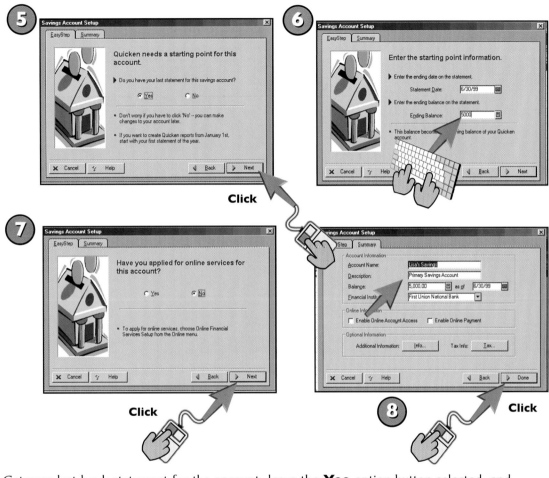

Entering an Account Number and Other Details

When the Savings Account Setup dialog box prompts you for an Account Name and Description, don't enter the account number. To enter the account number and other more detailed information, click the **Info** button on the Summary tab of the Savings Account Setup dialog box (see step 8). Fill in any text boxes you want in the Additional Account Information dialog box and click **OK**.

✔️ **To the List**
Click the **Accounts** QuickTab to display the Account List window. To return to the My Finances Center, click the **My Finances** QuickTab.

✔️ **Going Online**
See Part 6 to later set up an account for online banking.

⑤ Get your last bank statement for the account, leave the **Yes** option button selected, and click **Next**.

⑥ Enter the **Statement Date** and **Ending Balance** and click **Next**.

⑦ Leave the **No** option button selected when you're asked about online services and click **Next**.

⑧ Verify and correct the account information and then click **Done** to finish opening your new account.

Task 7: Using the Account List to Display an Account's Register

Displaying an Account

When you've created multiple accounts in Quicken, you need to ensure that you're working with the right account before you start entering information. If you selected the wrong account when you started Quicken, use the *Account List* to choose another account.

✓ Faster Openings

You also can double-click any account in the Account List to open that account. Right-click an account to display a shortcut menu with commands for deleting the account (Delete) or editing the account information (Edit).

✓ Controlling Quicken

You can customize many aspects of how Quicken works using the **Edit, Options** submenu choices. For example, use the **Quicken Program** choice to find options for the overall program.

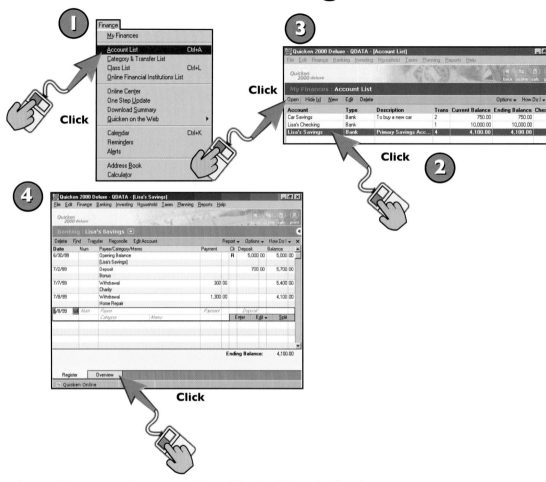

Start Here

Click

Click

Click

Click

Choose **Finance, Account List (Ctrl+A)** to display the Account List.

Click the account you want to open.

Click the **Open** button on the button bar to display the register window for the selected account.

Click the **Overview** tab at the bottom of the window to display the account overview.

Next Step

Using the Overview Tab

The Overview tab shows basic information about the account (Account Attributes and other statistics) and the current balance. You can click an Account Attributes entry to edit it. It also offers links you can click to perform activities such as reconciling the account with your bank statement or writing and printing checks.

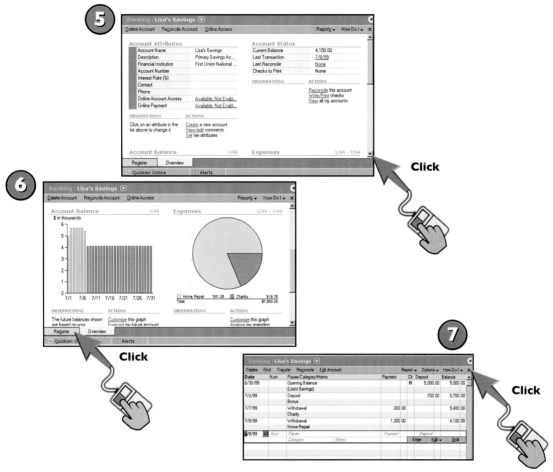

Click

Click

Click

Your Choice
The examples in this book show how to perform operations via menu commands, but you can use the account Overview.

Custom Views
You can customize the My Finances Center, Overview window, and many other windows and centers. Click a **Customize** link that appears onscreen to view customization choices.

⑤ Scroll down to view more Overview information.

⑥ Click the **Register** tab to return to the register of account information.

⑦ To close the register window, click the **Close** (**X**) button at the right end of its toolbar.

Tracking Income and Expenses

Perhaps you would like to know how much money you spend on various types of expenses (such as food, utilities, and car expenses) or where all of your money comes from (paycheck, odd jobs, rebates, and so on). Manually totaling such information could take hours a week. Instead, you can use a Quicken *category* or *subcategory* to identify an income source or expense for each transaction. Quicken comes with dozens of predefined categories and subcategories, but you also can add your own.

✓ Making More Groups

Groups classify similar categories and subcategories. To create a new group to contain categories, click the **New** button at the bottom of the **Group** drop-down list. Enter a **Group Name** in the **Create Category Group** dialog box and click **OK**.

Task 8: Creating a Category or Subcategory

Start Here

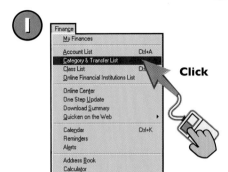

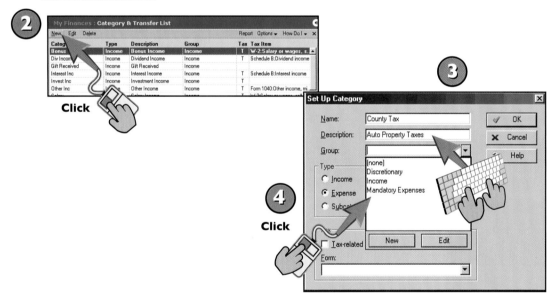

① Choose **Finance**, **Category & Transfer List** (**Ctrl+C**) to display the Category & Transfer List.

② Click the **New** button on the toolbar.

③ Enter a **Name** and **Description** for your new category or subcategory.

④ To select a group for the new category or subcategory, open the **Group** drop-down list and click a choice.

Next Step

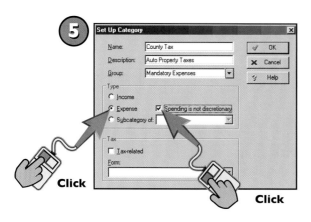

Click

Click

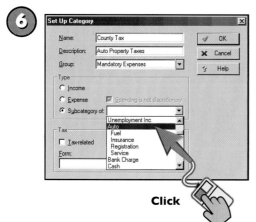

Click

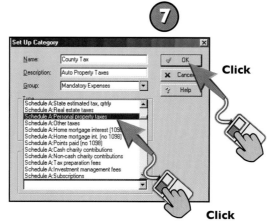

Click

Click

Adding Categories Even More Quickly

Quicken offers even more categories and subcategories than those initially listed in the Category & Transfer List. To add another existing category, choose **Finance, Category & Transfer List (Ctrl+C)** to display the Category & Transfer List. Click **Options** on the toolbar, and then click **Add Categories** in the menu that appears. Open the **Available Categories** drop-down list and click a choice to view categories of that type. To select a category, click it in the list of categories and click the **Add** button. When you finish adding categories, click **OK**.

5 Click either **Income** or **Expense** to identify the category's purpose. Also, if appropriate, check **Spending Is Not Discretionary**.

6 To create a subcategory, click the **Subcategory Of** option button, open the drop-down list, and click the category.

7 For a tax category, check **Tax-Related**, open the **Form** drop-down list, and click the appropriate tax form. Click **OK** to finish creating the category.

End Task

Using Quicken to Track Checks and Your Balance

Most users think of Quicken primarily as an electronic checkbook. While today's version offers so much more, Quicken Deluxe indeed provides you a lot of value even if you use it solely to enter and print checks. Each time you enter a check transaction into the register for a checking account, Quicken automatically recalculates the current *ending balance* for your account, making sure you always have a handle on what your spending limits are. Use the *new transaction line* to enter your new transaction.

(✓) **Postdating a Transaction**

To *postdate* a check so you can print it (or send the printed check) at a later time, enter a date that's in the future.

Task 9: Entering a Check

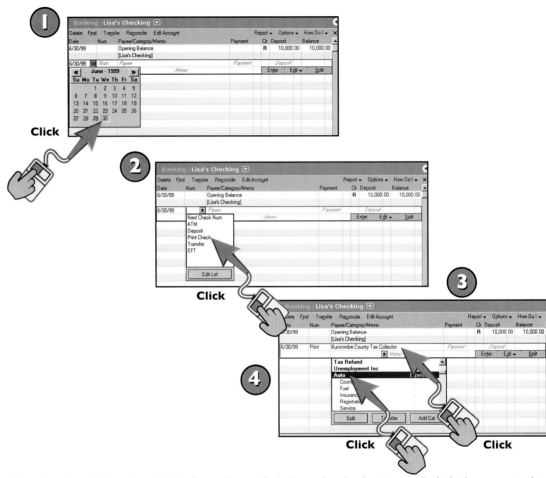

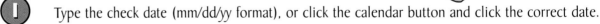

1. Type the check date (mm/dd/yy format), or click the calendar button and click the correct date.

2. Click the **Num** field and then click **Next Check Number** or **Print Check**. You can also type a specific check number in the Num field.

3. Click in the **Payee** field and type a payee name.

4. Click the **Category** field and select an expense category or subcategory.

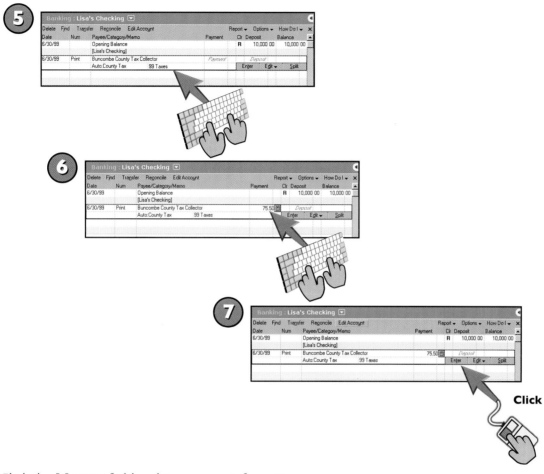

Synchronizing Checks

When entering a transaction for a check you've already written by hand, enter the correct check number in the **Num** field. If you select **Next Check Number** from the Num drop-down list, Quicken assigns the next available check number to the transaction and assumes you're writing the check by hand. If you select **Print Check**, Quicken calculates and enters the correct check number for each check, when printed. Task 19 explains how to print checks.

Click

✓ Click or Calculate an Amount

Clicking the button that appears in the Payment or Deposit field displays a calculator pad. Click its numbers and operators to enter or calculate an amount. Click the (=) Enter button to finish the entry.

(5) Click the **Memo** field and type memo information.

(6) Click the **Payment** field and type a payment amount.

(7) Click the **Enter** button below the new transaction line to finish entering the transaction.

Putting Money into an Account

The money you deposit into an account can come from your paycheck, interest deposited into your account by the bank, loose cash you deposit via an **ATM**, gifts you receive from relatives, and so on. Every time you deposit money into your account at a bank or **ATM**, be sure to enter a corresponding deposit transaction in the Quicken account for that checking, savings, or money market account. Enter a new deposit on the new transaction line for the account in the register.

ⓘ WARNING

When you enter a withdrawal (or deposit) transaction, make sure you don't type a number in the Num field. Quicken allows this, but doing so creates confusion with the check numbers you enter.

Task 10: Entering a Deposit

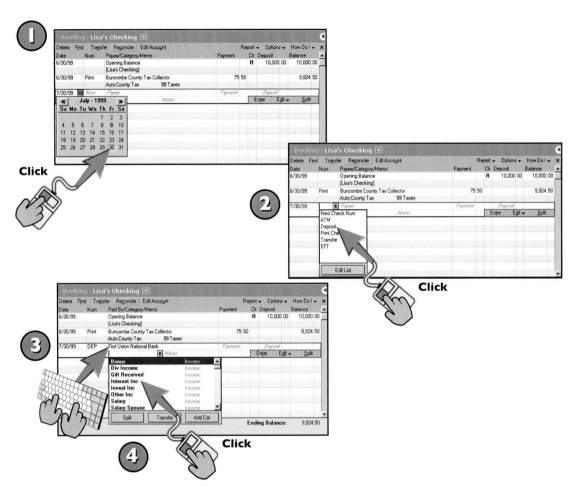

① Type the deposit date (mm/dd/yy format) or click the calendar button and click the correct date.

② Click the **Num** field and then click **Deposit** or **EFT** (if your employer deposits your paycheck electronically). EFT stands for Electronic Funds Transfer.

③ Click in the **Paid By** field and type the name of the person or company from which you received the funds.

④ Click the **Category** field and select an income category or subcategory.

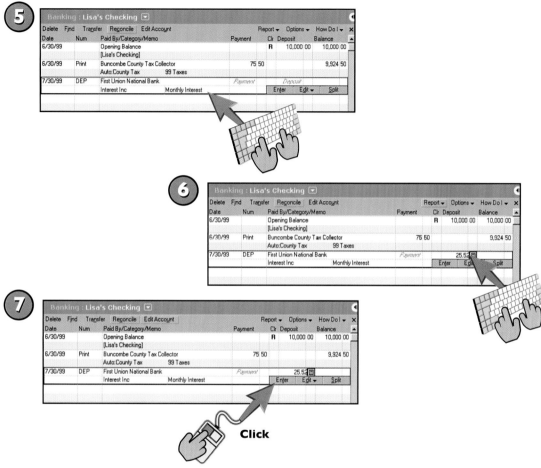

Click

Categorizing Your Income

Categorizing your income is just as important as categorizing your expenses, so don't skip the Category field for your deposit transactions.

ⓘ WARNING

Keep in mind that it might take a few days for a deposit to clear so the funds actually become available in your account. If you immediately write checks that bring your checking account balance below the amount it was before you made the deposit, you might bounce a check.

✓ Paycheck Time

If you categorize a deposit as Salary, a Paycheck Setup dialog box might ask whether you want to use that feature to automate your paycheck entries. For more information on using this feature, see Part 2, Task 14.

⑤ You can click the **Memo** field and type memo information, if you wish.

⑥ Click the **Deposit** field and specify a deposit amount.

⑦ Click the **Enter** button below the new transaction line to finish entering the transaction.

Task 11: Entering a Withdrawal

Taking Money Out of an Account

To keep track of withdrawals, use the new transaction line to enter a withdrawal, which resembles entering a check.

✓ Withdrawal Nums

The Num field doesn't include a withdrawal choice. To make one, open the **Num** field drop-down list and click **Edit List**. Click **New**, type an **Add to Num/Ref List** text box entry such as **WD** for Withdrawal, click **OK**, and click **Done**.

✓ List of Payees?

If you select the Payee field in any transaction and a list opens, it holds memorized transactions. See Part 2, Tasks 1–3, to learn how to work with memorized transactions. For now, simply type the entry you want.

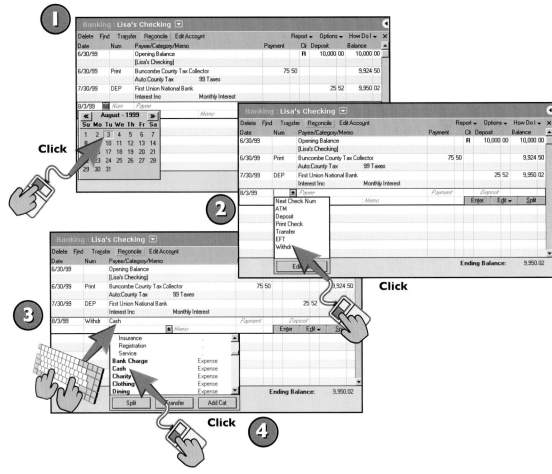

① Type the withdrawal date (mm/dd/yy format) or click the calendar button and click the correct date.

② Either skip the Num field, or click the **Num** field and click the name for the withdrawal choice you created.

③ Click the **Payee** field and type a payee name (the cash recipient or something generic such as **Cash**).

④ Click the **Category** field and select an expense category or subcategory.

Next Step

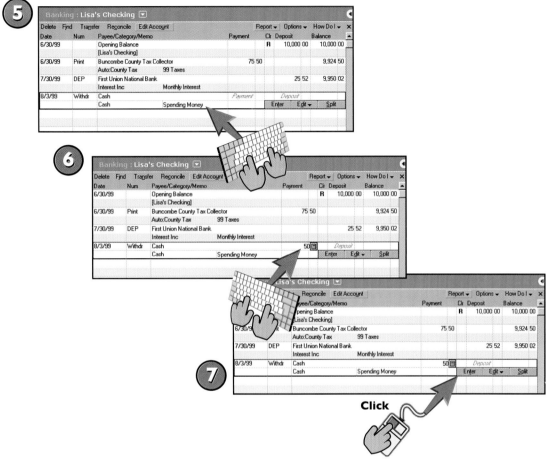

Categorizing Withdrawals

Quicken provides a category you can use for miscellaneous account withdrawals—the Cash expense category. Otherwise, you should choose the category that best reflects how you spent the money: Dining, Fuel (a subcategory of Auto), Gifts Given, and so on.

Click

5 Click the **Memo** field and type memo information.

6 Click the **Payment** field and specify a withdrawal amount.

7 Click the **Enter** button below the new transaction line to finish entering the transaction.

Tracking Your Bank Machine Visits

Bank machines or ATMs provide a huge amount of freedom for all of us. We can walk up to an ATM at any hour of the day and make a deposit or withdraw the cash we need from a checking or savings account. With freedom comes responsibility, however, and many of us have fallen short in terms of tracking our ATM withdrawals. Because Quicken Deluxe eases the pain of entering ATM transactions, you should begin making your entries now to improve your financial management. Enter a new deposit on the new transaction line for the account in the Register.

✓ **Tossing Your Receipts?**
Don't trash your ATM withdrawal receipts. Use those receipts as the basis for ATM transactions you enter into Quicken.

Task 12: Entering an ATM Withdrawal or Deposit

Start Here

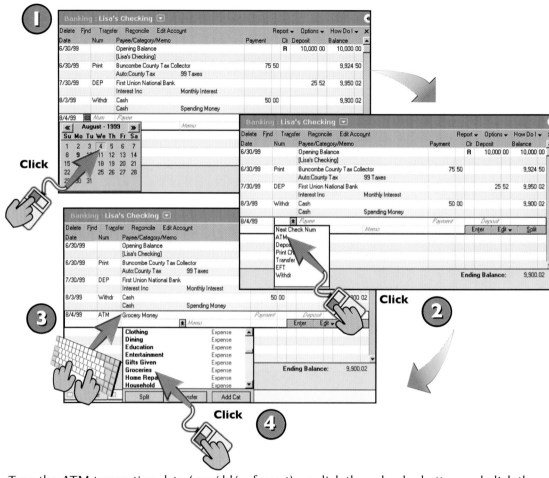

Click

Click

Click

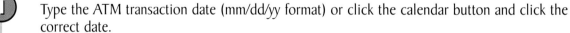

① Type the ATM transaction date (mm/dd/yy format) or click the calendar button and click the correct date.

② Click the **Num** field and then click **ATM**.

③ Click the **Payee** field and type a payee name (the cash recipient, something generic such as **Cash**, or the deposit source).

④ Click the **Category** field and select an expense category (perhaps **Cash**) or subcategory.

Next Step

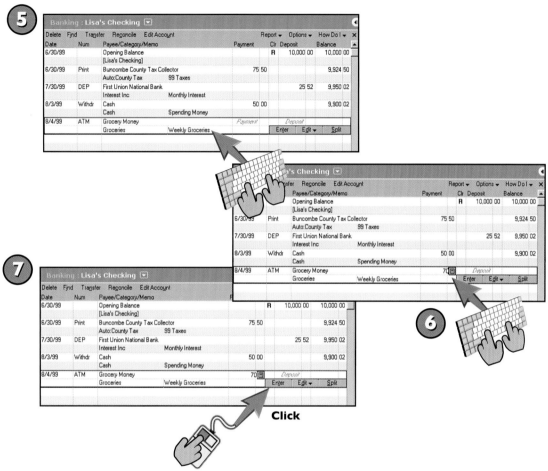

Click

Entering ATM Fees

Depending on the type of account you have, you might incur a fee each time you use your **ATM**. If you use an **ATM** from another bank, you can guarantee you're generating a fee. If you're using your bank's **ATM**, you might be able to accurately include the **ATM** fee as part of the **ATM** transaction; however, to ensure you're entering accurate **ATM** fees, you should wait until you receive your bank statement and enter a separate transaction for each fee.

⑤ Click the **Memo** field and type memo information.

⑥ Click the **Payment** field or **Deposit** field and specify an amount.

⑦ Click the **Enter** button below the new transaction line to finish entering the transaction.

Moving Your Money

Many of us end up with
multiple bank accounts.
People typically have both a
checking and a savings
account to earn interest on
at least part of their
deposits. You might have
multiple savings accounts—
one for yourself and spouse
and one for each of your
kids. When you move
money from one account to
another, you're transferring
the money; for example,
you might *transfer* money
from your savings account
to your checking account to
ensure you can cover a
check. Create a transfer
transaction in Quicken to
account for the money you
moved between bank
accounts.

✓ **Another Quicken Account**

To complete a transfer, you
have to have more that
one account created within
Quicken Deluxe. Return to
Task 6 to learn how to add
an account.

Task 13: Transferring Funds Between Accounts

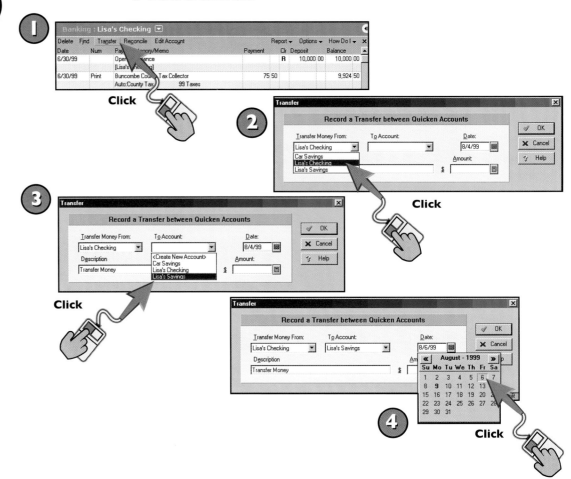

Click

Click

Click

Click

① Click the **Transfer** button on the toolbar for the register window for any account.

② From the **Transfer Money From** drop-down list in the Transfer dialog box, select the account from which to transfer funds.

③ From the **To Account** drop-down list, select the account into which you want to move the money.

④ Type the transfer transaction date (mm/dd/yy format) or click the calendar button and click the correct date.

Next Step

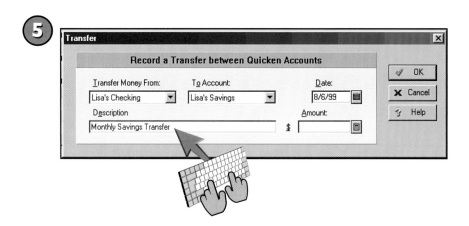

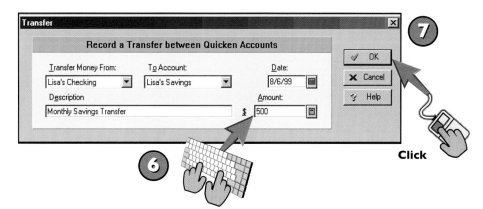

Although you can't assign a category or subcategory to a transfer transaction, it's still important to use the Description text box to capture information. For example, if you make a large transfer from savings to checking to make a tax payment, you could enter a description such as "99 Taxes." If you're transferring money to a child's account for educational costs, you can make an entry such as "March school allowance." Such record-keeping enables you to go back and verify when you've made a needed transfer for a particular purpose.

⑤ Edit the contents of the **Description** text box, if needed.

⑥ Click the **Amount** text box and type or specify an amount.

⑦ Click **OK** to finish entering the transaction.

Click

✓ Recording a Transfer
Quicken Deluxe creates two transaction entries for the transfer—one in the account from which you transferred the money and one in the account to which you transferred the money.

Task 14: Splitting a Transaction

Assigning Multiple Categories

Our activities in life don't often fall neatly into categories—neither do our financial transactions. When you write a check, it might cover one expense or several different ones, such as when the check you're writing is to pay a credit card bill. To handle such situations, Quicken enables you to *split* a transaction. When you split a transaction in a bank account, you apply more than one category or subcategory and specify what portion of the transaction falls in each category or subcategory.

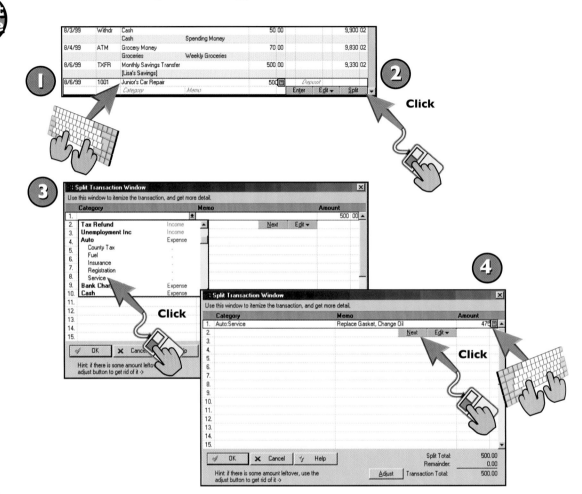

1. Fill in the **Date**, **Num**, **Payee**, and **Payment** (or **Deposit**) fields for the new transaction you want to split.

2. Click the **Split** button below the new transaction line.

3. In the first empty line of the Split Transaction Window dialog box, select a category from the **Category** drop-down list.

4. Type **Memo** and **Amount** entries and click **Next**.

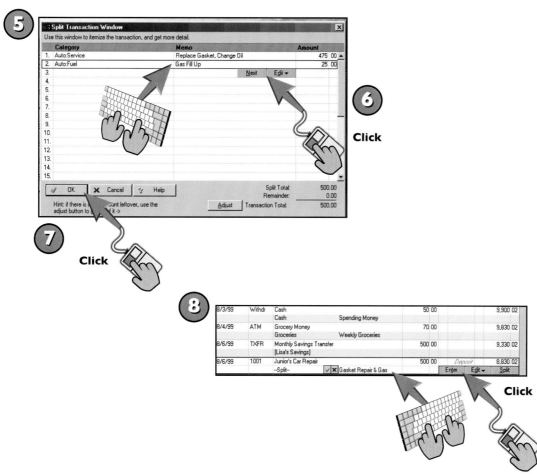

Adjusting the Transaction

If you're entering a Quicken transaction before you make the real transaction, you might find the initial transaction payment or deposit amount you entered is too high or low, based on the categorized amounts. Say you're making a cash withdrawal to cover a few anticipated expenses, and you initially enter $100 for the transaction. You split the transaction as follows: Dining $40, Groceries $50, and Cash $20, which adds up to $110. In such a case, click the **Adjust** button in the Split Transaction Window dialog box to have Quicken calculate the correct payment or deposit amount.

5 Specify the next **Category** and **Memo**. Edit the **Amount** entry or simply continue if the calculated amount is correct.

6 Click **Next** and repeat step 5 as many times as necessary to add other categories.

7 Click **OK** to finish entering the categories for the split and return to the register.

8 Enter a transaction **Memo** and click the **Enter** button below the new transaction line to finish entering the transaction.

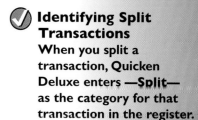

Identifying Split Transactions
When you split a transaction, Quicken Deluxe enters —Split— as the category for that transaction in the register.

Task 15: Editing a Transaction

Changing Transaction Information

You can edit a transaction to change the payment or deposit amount, the category, or some other field. For example, if you enter a payment in advance of receiving its bill, you might need to go back and adjust the payment amount before you print the check. Make transaction changes in the register.

✓ Using the Edit Button

For other changes, click the transaction and click the **Edit** button below it. Click the **Delete Transaction** choice and **Yes** to remove the selected transaction from the register.

⚠ WARNING

Avoid changing a *cleared transaction.* When you do change a cleared transaction, Quicken asks you to verify the change. See Part 3, Tasks 1–5, to learn more.

Start Here

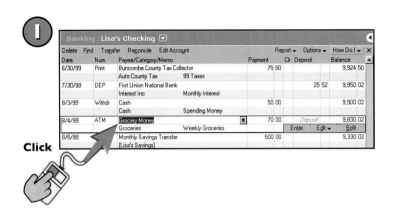

Click

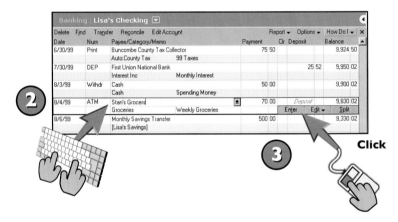

Click

1 Scroll the register, find the transaction you want to edit, and click any field in the transaction to select it.

2 Make your changes to the transaction fields, as needed.

3 Click the **Enter** button below the transaction line to finish entering the changes, or press **Esc** to cancel editing.

End Task

Task 16: Voiding a Transaction

Start Here

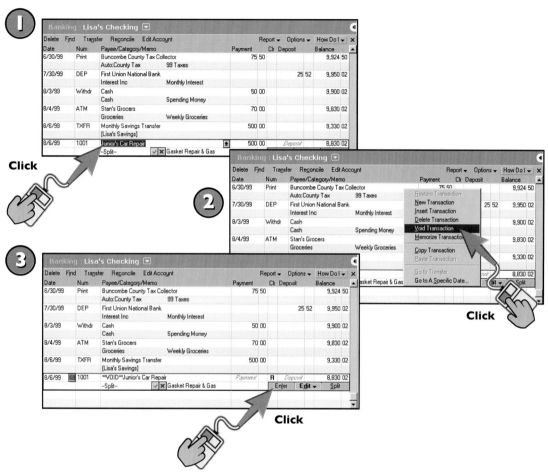

Telling Quicken about Invalidated Checks

If you stop a payment because a check gets lost in the mail or a recipient refuses to cash a check, you need to **void** the transaction. Voiding a check leaves the its number and transaction in the register. This helps Quicken correctly number later checks and helps you account for the gap between valid check numbers. Quicken inserts ****VOID**** in the Payee field for a voided check and marks the check as cleared. Void a check in the register.

1 Scroll the register, find the transaction you want to void, and click any field in the transaction to select it.

2 Click the **Edit** button below the transaction and then click **Void Transaction**.

3 Click the **Enter** button below the transaction line to finish voiding the transaction.

WARNING
Quicken doesn't offer an Undo feature to let you reinstate a check you've voided.

Task 17: Finding a Check or Transaction

Searching for the Transaction You Need

After a few months or so, you might accumulate quite a few transactions in a Quicken Deluxe account, particularly a checking account. When you need to double-check or change the information in a transaction, you can use the Find feature to jump to the transaction you need. When you perform a Find, you enter information that appears in the transaction, such as a specific check number. Quicken Deluxe takes you to the matching transaction in the register.

✅ **Controlling Search Precision**
Use the **Match If** choice to specify how narrow or broad the find operation should be. The **Exactly** choice narrows results most—found transactions must match exactly with this selected.

Click

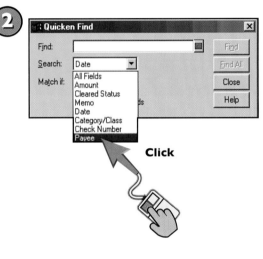

Click

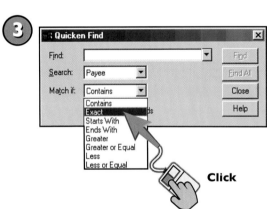

Click

Start Here

① Click the **Find** button on the toolbar.

② From the **Search** drop-down list in the Quicken Find dialog box, select the type of information to match.

③ Select an operator from the **Match If** list.

Next Step

Finding Multiple Matching Transactions

You might have multiple transactions spread through different accounts that match the Find criteria you specify. You can click the **Find All** button in the Quicken Find dialog box to display a window listing all matching records in the current account and other accounts in the same Quicken file. To go to a particular matching transaction in the register, double-click the transaction in the list of matching transactions.

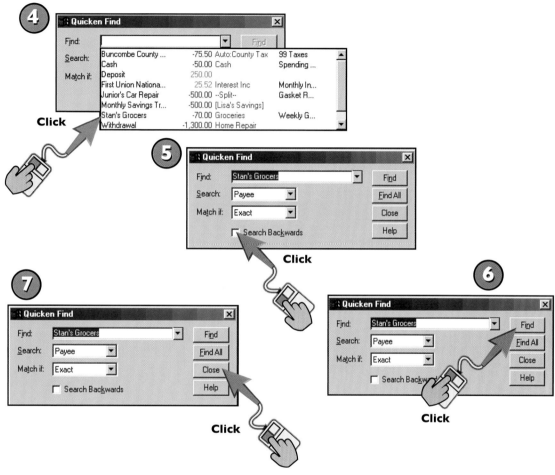

Click

Click

Click

Click

✓ **Finding Again**
The Quicken Find dialog box remembers your last search settings. If you closed the Quicken Find dialog box, you can click **Find** on the toolbar to redisplay your find choices.

✓ **No More Matches**
Quicken displays a message if it can't find any more matching records.

(4) Specify the information to match by typing it into the **Find** text box or by selecting from the text box's list.

(5) To search forward through the register, clear the **Search Backwards** check box.

(6) Click **Find** to jump to the first matching record in the register. Repeat to find subsequent matches.

(7) Click **Close** to finish the Find and work with the found transaction.

Task 18: Sorting Transactions and Adjusting the Transaction List

Sorting the Register

By default, the register organizes transactions according to the transaction date. It further sorts transactions on the current date in order of amount, from largest to smallest. You might want to display the transactions in another order, instead. For example, you might want to sort the transactions by payee, so you can review recent payments to that payee.

✓ Today's Dateline

If you enter one or more postdated transactions, a blue highlight line appears above the first postdated transaction. The line sets off the postdated or future transactions from the current transactions.

⚠ WARNING

Some sorting orders cause your balance to calculate incorrectly, so return to the original sort order to get an accurate balance calculation.

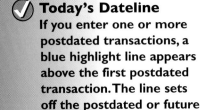

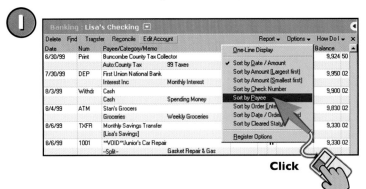

Click

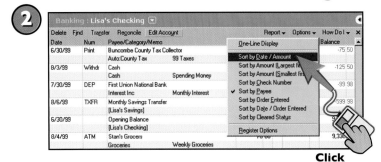

Click

Click

1 Click the **Options** button on the toolbar, and then click the new sort order to use.

2 To return to the original order, click the **Options** button on the toolbar and click **Sort by Date/Amount**.

3 Click the **Options** button on the toolbar, and then click **One-Line Display**.

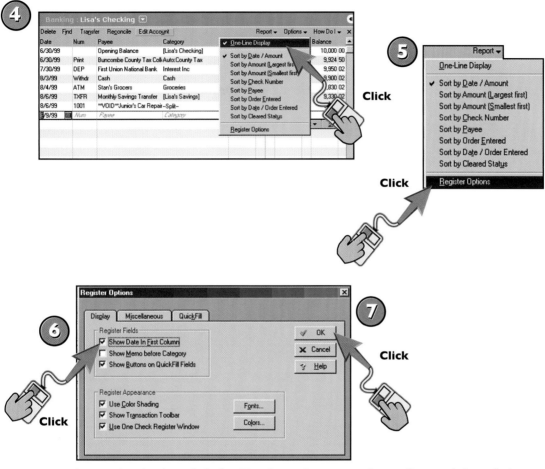

Controlling the Register List

You can make further changes to how the register displays transactions and behaves by clicking the **Options** button and using other commands. You can hide some transaction information so each transaction only requires a single line, including more transactions onscreen or in a printout. Use the Register Options command to control register appearance and behavior settings, such as its color.

Click

Click

Click

Click

④ To return to the regular display, click the **Options** button on the toolbar, and then click **One-Line Display** again.

⑤ Click the **Options** button on the toolbar, and then click **Register Options**.

⑥ Make the choices you want in the Register Options dialog box.

⑦ Click **OK** to Close the dialog box.

✓ **As You Like It**
There are 20 different options for adjusting how the register looks and works, including whether or not Quicken memorizes transaction information you enter. Quicken organizes these options on three tabs—Display, Miscellaneous, and QuickFill—in the Register Options dialog box.

Task 19: Printing Checks

Setting Up the Printer

Printing checks in Quicken Deluxe consists of two stages: getting checks and then setting up your printer for them and actually printing. If you've decided to print checks from Quicken, go to `www.IntuitMarketPlace.com` or check the catalog that came with Quicken. After you've selected the style of check to use and have received your checks, you should follow the printer setup process to ensure your checks print correctly.

✓ Printing Test

To print test checks on blank paper, choose **File, Printer Setup, For Printing Checks.** Click **Align** and click a check alignment button. Next, click **Print Sample.** Use a choice in the Fine Alignment dialog box to correct alignment, if needed.

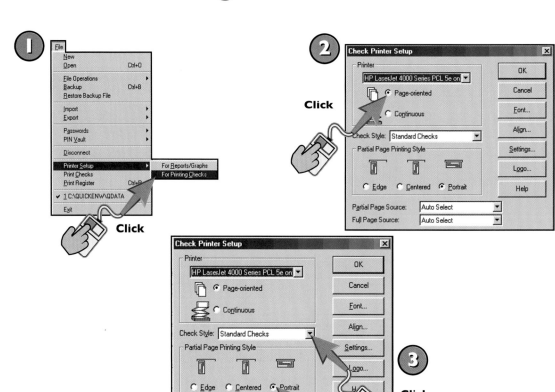

Start Here

Click

Click

Click

Click

1 Choose **File**, **Printer Setup**, **For Printing Checks**.

2 Select a printer from the **Printer** drop-down list. Choose **Page-Oriented** or **Continuous** for the printer's paper type.

3 Select the type of checks you purchased from the **Check Style** drop-down list.

4 Select a choice in the **Partial Page Printing Style** area and click **OK** to finish specifying print settings.

Next Step

Finishing the Print Job

After you've set up your printer and tested the printout, you can load up your printer with your new checks and get going. Quicken Deluxe prints every check transaction displaying Print in the Num field. It numbers the checks sequentially, starting with a number you specify during the print process. After you print the check(s), the assigned check number(s) appear in the Num field in the register.

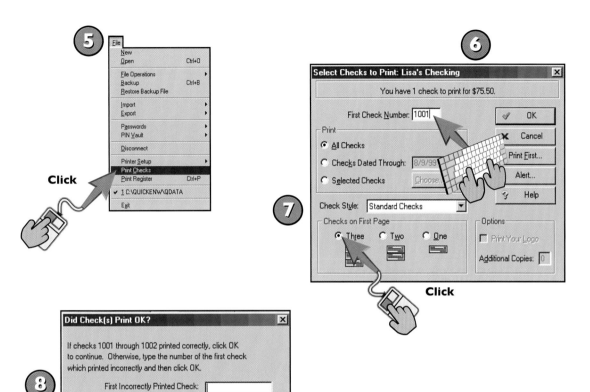

Click

Click

Click

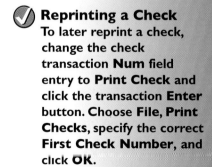

⑤ While displaying the register for the account with the checks to print, choose **File**, **Print Checks**.

⑥ In the **First Check Number** text box, enter the check number to use for the first printed check.

⑦ If the first page of checks is partial, make a choice in the **Checks on First Page** area. Click **OK**.

⑧ After the checks print, click **OK** when the Did Check(s) Print OK? message box appears.

✓ **Reprinting a Check**
To later reprint a check, change the check transaction **Num** field entry to **Print Check** and click the transaction **Enter** button. Choose **File, Print Checks**, specify the correct **First Check Number**, and click **OK**.

End Task

Task 20: Printing the Register

Seeing Your Transactions on Paper

The register gives you detailed information about each transaction in your account, so you can check the account history any time you want. For example, if you want to review recent transactions for an account with your spouse or a financial planning professional, you can print the relevant transactions from the register rather than huddling around your computer. Display the register for the account with the transactions to print, sort the transactions in the order you prefer, and then continue as described here.

✓ When to Print

You don't have to print your account every week or month to have a safe copy of your data. Instead, back up your Quicken file on disk, as described in Task 22.

Click

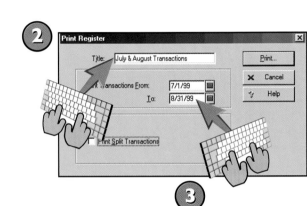

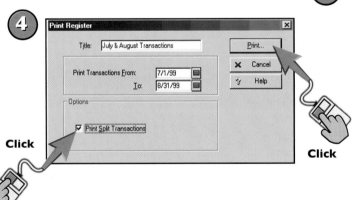

Click

Click

Start Here

(1) Choose **File**, **Print Register (Ctrl+P)**.

(2) In the **Title** text box, type the phrase that you want to display at the top of the printout.

(3) To print only transactions with date entries from a particular period, change the **From** and **To** text box entries.

(4) If you want to include all of the category information for split transactions, check **Print Split Transactions**. Click **Print**.

Next Step

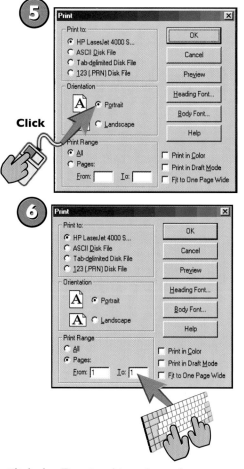

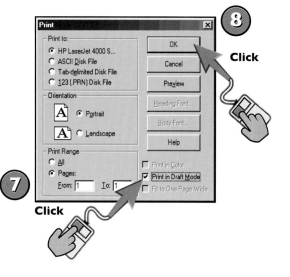

Controlling the Printout

The **Print** dialog box offers a number of settings you can use to fine-tune the look of your printed report. In addition to those described in this task, you can use the **Heading Font** and **Body Font** buttons to display dialog boxes in which you can change the fonts used for your printout by making choices from the **Font, Font Style,** and **Size** lists. Click **OK** to return to the Print dialog box. Click the **Preview** button to check out your printout, and click **Close** to return to the Print dialog box.

(5) Click the **Portrait** or **Landscape** orientation option button.

(6) To print selected pages only, click **Pages** and enter the first and last page in the **From** and **To** text boxes.

(7) Choose any other print options that apply

(8) Click **OK**.

✔️ **Is It a Report?**
Printing the register is not the same as printing a Quicken *report*. For more about reports, see part 3. Task 8 in that Part explains how to print a report.

End
Task

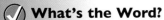

Task 21: Adding a Password to Protect Your Quicken Data

Protecting a File with a Password

Financial fraud can become a problem for anyone who's not careful with personal financial information. For example, if you've included an account number among the information you entered for a Quicken account, someone could steal that number and use it to obtain money or charge goods and services. Adding a password to your Quicken file prevents others from taking a look at your accounts. A password can be up to 16 characters and can include spaces, but capitalization doesn't matter.

✓ What's the Word?

You have to choose a password carefully. Too obvious, and others can guess it. Too obscure, and you'll forget it. Steer clear of family names or numbers. Instead use a favorite thing, such as a song title.

Start Here

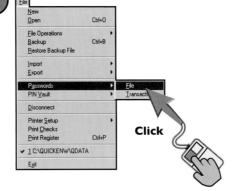

Click

Click

① Choose **File**, **Passwords**, **File**.

② Enter the password twice—in the **Password** and **Confirm Password** text boxes.

③ Click **OK** to finish assigning the password.

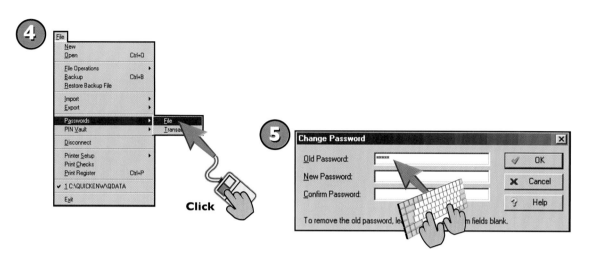

Changing or Removing the Password

When a file already includes a password, you can change or remove that password at any time. You have to use the old password to change passwords, though, so don't forget it. If you have a lot of visitors in your home or use Quicken on a notebook computer that you also carry to work, it wouldn't hurt to change your password every month or so to safeguard your privacy. If you find a password too cumbersome, you can remove it altogether. Here's how to remove a password from the current file.

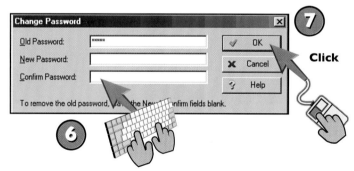

4 Choose **File**, **Passwords**, **File**.

5 Enter the old password in the **Old Password** text box.

6 Enter the new password in the **New Password** and **Confirm Password** text boxes. Leave these blank to remove the old password.

7 Click **OK**.

✓ **Password, Please**
When a Quicken file has a password, the Quicken Password dialog box appears when you start Quicken or open the file. Enter the password in the **Password** text box. Click **OK** to open the file.

End Task

Task 22: Backing Up Your Quicken Data

Creating a Backup File

Disks work reliably until they become old or damaged. In addition, your old friend "human error" can corrupt a file. You should create a backup copy of your Quicken data file to ensure you can recover your transactions if something happens to your hard disk or data file. If you want to create the backup file on a floppy disk, insert a blank, formatted floppy disk into your floppy disk drive. The backup steps preserve the data for the current (active) Quicken file.

✓ **Choose Your Disk**

You can back up to either a hard disk or a floppy disk. I recommend doing both each time you back up. Follow the process to create a backup on floppy; repeat to create a hard disk backup. Label the floppy with the backup date.

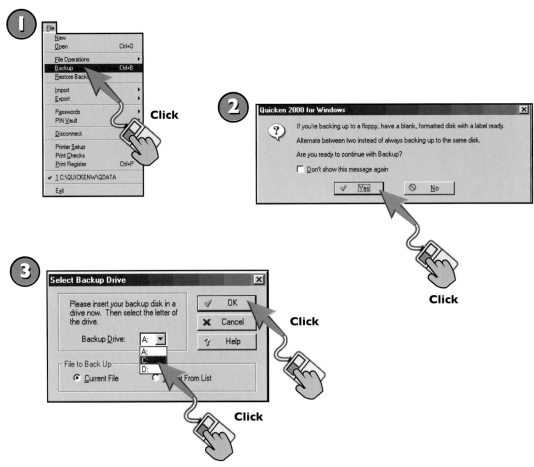

Insert a blank, formatted floppy disk if needed and choose **File**, **Backup (Ctrl+B)**.

Click **Yes** when asked if you're ready to continue the backup.

Choose the appropriate disk from the **Backup Drive** drop-down list and click **OK**.

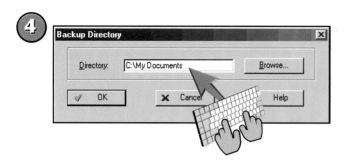

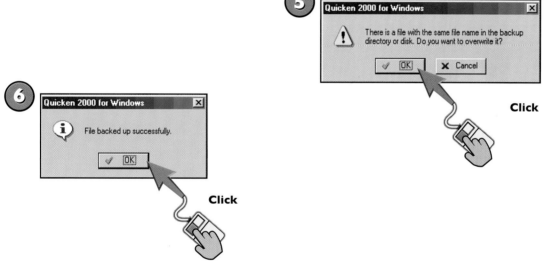

Click

Click

Backup Frequency

You should back up at least once a month, after you reconcile your main checking account with your statement. However, if you have a lot of accounts or enter many transactions per week, it's not unreasonable to back up weekly.

④ If prompted, enter or edit the backup folder name in the **Directory** text box and click **OK**.

⑤ If the backup disk or folder already holds a backup of the current file, click **OK** to overwrite the old backup.

⑥ Click **OK** at the message that tells you the backup is complete.

How Did I Get Home?
After you back up or restore the Quicken data file, Quicken displays the My Finances Center. From there, you'll need to redisplay the register or navigate to any other feature you'd like to use.

Restoring a Backup File to Recover Your Data

If your hard disk or Quicken data file goes on the fritz, you can rest easy if you have a recent backup file, because you can simply restore that backup file. The restored data overwrites any current version of the backed-up file that's open. You might have to update or add a few recent transactions, but that beats retyping everything or just starting a new file without your old transaction data. If your backup file is on a floppy disk, insert the floppy in the floppy disk drive and get started.

Task 23: Restoring Your Quicken Data

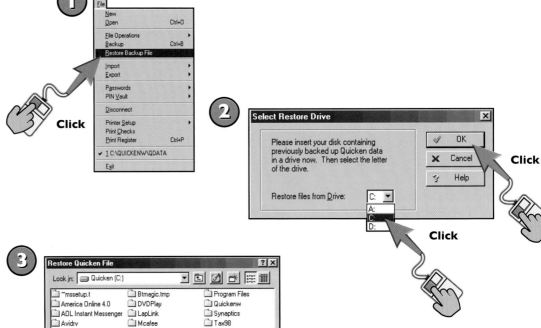

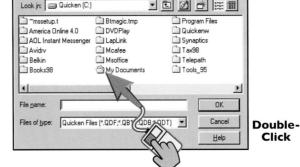

1   Choose **File**, **Restore Backup File**.

2   Select the disk that holds the backup file from the **Restore Files from Drive** drop-down list. Click **OK**.

3   If prompted, select the folder that holds your backup file.

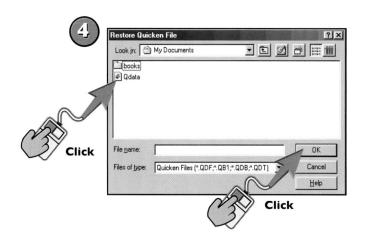

Selecting the Backup

The backup filename matches the name of the original file, such as Qdata.qdf. Quicken just places the backup file in a different location than the original. If you've stored backup copies for multiple Quicken files in the same location, be careful to select the right one.

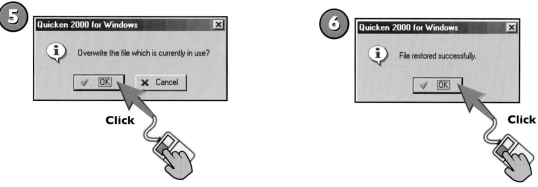

(4) Click the backup file you want to use (probably Qdata.qdf) and then click **OK**.

(5) Click **OK** at the message that asks if you want to overwrite the current file.

(6) Click **OK** at the message that tells you the restore operation worked.

✓ **File It**
See the first three tasks in Part 7 to learn how to create and work with Quicken files.

PART 2

Speeding Up Your Transaction Entries

You might be thinking that using Quicken Deluxe 2000 causes you to swap tedious hours of handwriting checks for tedious hours of typing transactions at your computer. Not so! This part introduces you to features and tricks you can use to streamline Quicken entries. After you take a little time to set things up, Quicken rewards you by doing even more of your work.

Tasks

Using a Memorized Transaction

As noted in Part 1, each time you enter a transaction using a new payee, Quicken remembers the transaction information and creates a *memorized transaction*, adding that transaction to the *Memorized Transaction List.* Any time you need that payee again, you can use the *QuickFill* feature to enter a copy of the transaction information and then update the information to create a new entry in your register.

✓ **Less Is More**

Sometimes QuickFill displays only a single transaction in a yellow pop-up box above the Payee field rather than a list of multiple transactions. Just keep typing until the correct transaction information appears, and then press the **Tab** key to continue.

Task 1: Using QuickFill with New Transactions

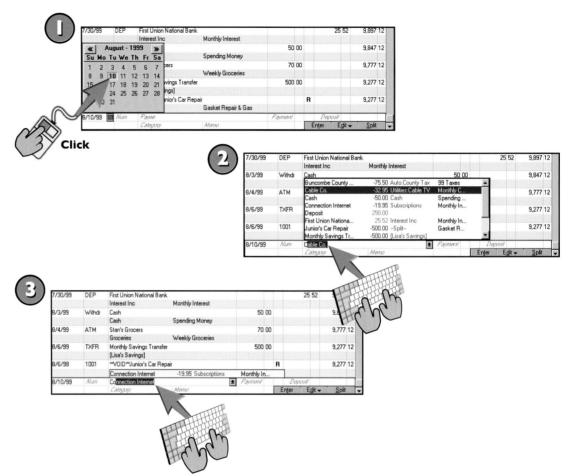

Click

---

1 Type the check date (m/dd/yy format), or click the **Calendar** button and click the correct date.

2 Click in the **Payee** field and begin typing a payee name.

3 Continue typing until the correct payee name is highlighted, and then press **Tab**.

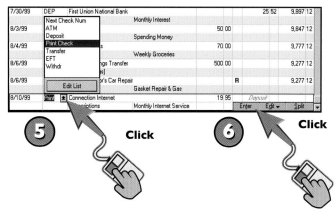

Turning Off QuickFill

You don't have to leave the QuickFill feature on. If you often write checks to payees whom you'll never pay again, the Memorized Transaction List can actually become so long that it'd be cumbersome to use. To turn off QuickFill, open the **Options** menu on the register window toolbar and choose **Register Options.** Click the **QuickFill** tab, clear the **Auto Memorize New Transactions** check box, and then click **OK.**

Click

Click

① **WARNING**
If the transaction corresponds with a monthly bill, be sure to check the amount due. The amount might vary by a few cents, or the payee might have added an increase or a fee. Your transaction payment entry must match the amount due.

④ Change the **Payment**, **Category**, and **Memo** field entries, if needed.

⑤ Adjust the **Num** field selection, if needed.

⑥ Click the **Enter** button below the transaction to finish entering it.

Task 2: Displaying and Sorting the Memorized Transaction List

Viewing Saved Transaction Information

When Quicken memorizes a payee and the accompanying transaction information, it places that information on your Memorized Transaction List. You can display the list to view and work with your memorized transactions. While the list is displayed, you can sort it to put the transactions in a different order.

✓ **What's Your Name?**
The Description column shows the entry you made in either the Payee or Paid By field. It is memorized by QuickFill, depending on the transaction type.

✓ **Using a Transaction**
Click a transaction in the Memorized Transaction List, and then click the **Use** button on the toolbar to insert a copy of that transaction in the currently open account register. Or, double-click the transaction to use it.

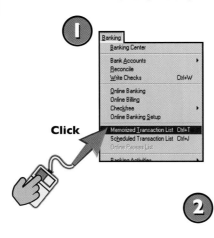

Click

Click

Click

① Choose **Banking**, **Memorized Transaction List** (**Ctrl+T**).

② Click **Options** on the toolbar and choose a new sort order for the list.

③ To return to the original sort order, click **Options** on the toolbar and choose **Sort by Description**.

Click

④ Click the Memorized Transaction List window **Close** (**X**) button.

Closing the Memorized Transaction List

When you've finished working with the Memorized Transaction List, you can close it to reduce the number of open windows. This makes navigating among Quicken features a little easier.

✓ **QuickTab List Close**
If you have the QuickTabs column displayed, you could right-click the **Transactions** choice, and then click **Close: Transactions** to close the Memorized Transactions List.

✓ **Adding a Transaction**
You can create a new transaction in the Memorized Transaction List window. Click the **New** button on the window toolbar, fill in the transaction information in the Create Memorized Transaction dialog box, and click **OK**.

End Task

Changing Saved Transaction Information

You can edit a transaction in the Memorized Transaction List. The next time you use QuickFill to use a copy of the memorized transaction, the transaction displays the edited information. Although the Memorized Transaction List can hold up to 2,000 transactions, you can keep Quicken lean and mean by deleting old transactions from time to time.

Task 3: Editing or Deleting a Memorized Transaction

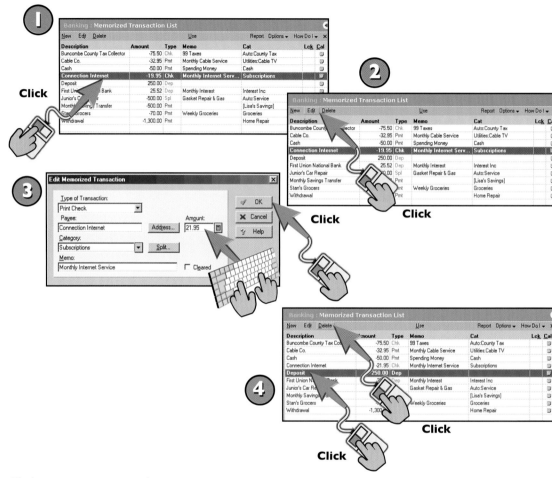

⚠️ **WARNING**
You cannot undo your changes to a memorized transaction or recall a memorized transaction if you delete it, so be sure you're making the change you want before you begin.

① Click a transaction to select it.

② To edit the transaction, click **Edit** on the toolbar.

③ Make any changes you want to the transaction information and click **OK**.

④ To delete a transaction, select it and then click **Delete** on the toolbar.

(5)

Click

(6)

Click

(7)

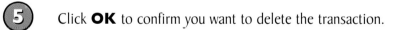

Click

Locking and Unlocking a Transaction

Suppose you use QuickFill to reuse a memorized transaction, and you make a slight change to the transaction, such as changing the Payment amount. Generally, Quicken also makes that change to the memorized transaction. To prevent any changes to a transaction, you can lock the transaction in the Memorized Transaction List. Later you can unlock the transaction if you need to change it. By default, new transactions are not locked, but transactions you add directly in the Memorized Transaction List are.

---

(5) Click **OK** to confirm you want to delete the transaction.

(6) To lock a transaction, click the **Lck** column for the transaction row.

(7) To unlock a transaction, click the **Lock** icon in the Lck column for the transaction row.

End Task

Task 4: Entering Transactions in QuickEntry 2000

Using QuickEntry Rather Than Quicken

In Quicken, navigating to the feature you want might slow you down. If all you want to do is enter a few quick transactions, you can use a program that presents only your account register and a limited number of commands—QuickEntry 2000. QuickEntry 2000 opens the Quicken data file you were using when you last opened Quicken and displays all of the accounts in that file. It displays the Ending Balance for each account, but not its transactions. You use the same procedure for entering a transaction in QuickEntry 2000 that you use in Quicken.

✓ Memorized Transactions

QuickEntry 2000 enables you to use any of your memorized transactions, just as you would in the register of the full Quicken program.

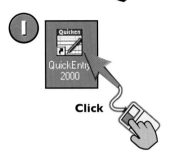

Click

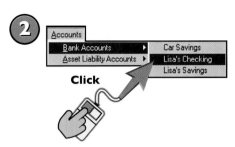

Click

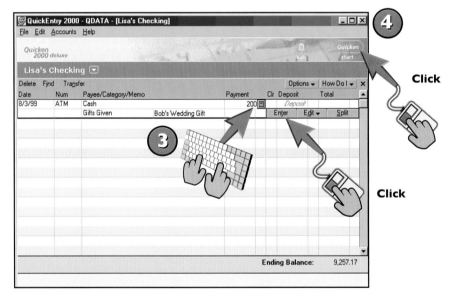

Click

Click

Double-click the **QuickEntry 2000** shortcut icon on the desktop.

To choose another account, choose **Accounts**, **Bank Accounts** (or **Accounts**, **Asset Liability Accounts**), and click the name of the account to use.

Enter one or more transactions.

If needed, click the **Quicken Start** button to start Quicken.

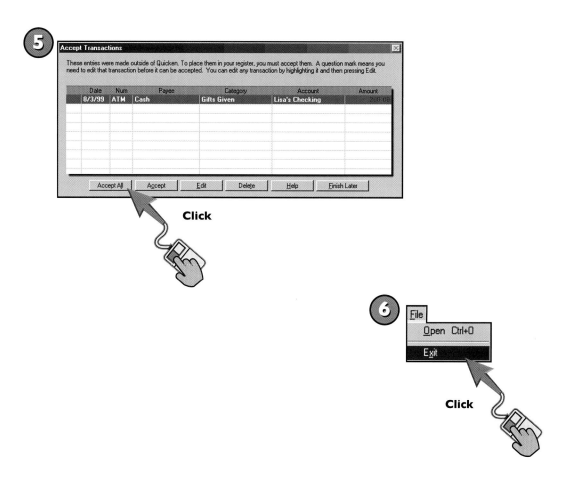

Click

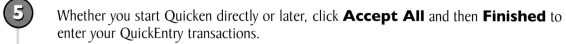

Click

Exiting QuickEntry

QuickEntry 2000 has a lot of limitations. It doesn't show you all of an account's transactions. It doesn't let you print anything, make a budget, view a graph, or do anything fancy. After you've used QuickEntry 2000, you might want to jump to the full Quicken program to finish up, or you might simply want to exit QuickEntry and do your heavy financial lifting on another day.

✅ Where Are My Transactions?
Each time you use QuickEntry 2000, it transfers the transaction information to Quicken, where you can accept or reject the entries. The next time you start QuickEntry 2000, it presents a blank register.

⑤ Whether you start Quicken directly or later, click **Accept All** and then **Finished** to enter your QuickEntry transactions.

⑥ Choose **File**, **Exit** to shut down the QuickEntry program instead of opening Quicken immediately.

✅ Another Start
You also can choose Start, Programs, Quicken, QuickEntry 2000 to launch QuickEntry 2000.

End Task

Task 5: Creating a Scheduled Transaction

Entering a Recurring Transaction

A *scheduled transaction* helps you remember when to enter a transaction to be paid. You can create a scheduled transaction for anything that happens at regular intervals. Quicken reminds you of each scheduled transaction and can even enter the transaction for you. Use the *Scheduled Transaction List* to create and manage scheduled transactions.

✅ **Date and Amount**
Your Next Date entry specifies the first date Quicken should use, for the scheduled transaction. Negative Amount entries reverse the transaction, so be careful.

✅ **It's Memorized**
You can use information from a memorized transaction by clicking the drop-down list arrow beside the **Payee** text box (in the Create Scheduled Transaction dialog box) and then clicking the memorized transaction.

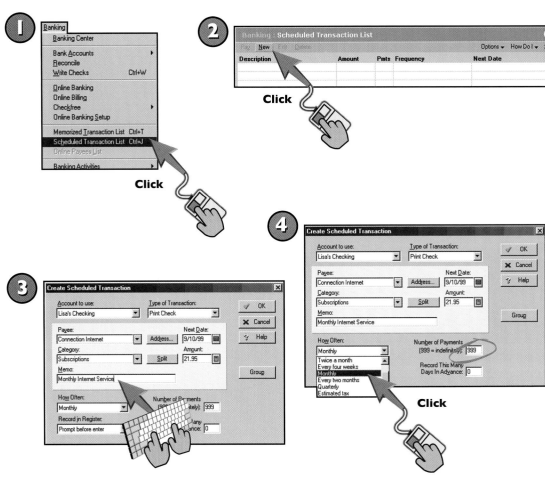

1 Choose **Banking**, **Scheduled Transaction List (Ctrl+J)**.

2 Click the **New** button on the Scheduled Transaction List toolbar.

3 Select or specify the **Account to Use**, **Type of Transaction**, **Payee**, **Next Date**, **Category**, **Amount**, and **Memo**.

4 Specify **How Often** Quicken should schedule the transaction and the **Number of Payments** to schedule.

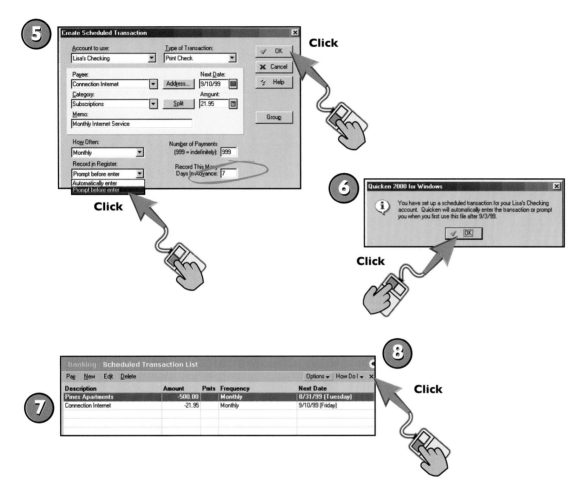

Click

Click

Click

Click

Click

Looking at Some of the Options

To print a check, choose **Print Check** from the **Type of Transaction** drop-down list. Choose **Two Weeks** from the **How Often** drop-down list for a biweekly paycheck. Set **Number of Payments** to 48 for 48 upcoming car payments. If you tell Quicken to record a payment automatically (by choosing **Automatically Enter** from the **Record in Register** drop-down list), tell it how far in advance by using the **Record This Many Days In Advance** text box.

⑤ Make a **Record in Register** choice and adjust the **Record This Many Days In Advance** entry, and then click **OK**.

⑥ If prompted, click **OK** to confirm the new scheduled transaction.

⑦ Repeat steps 2–6 as needed to schedule more transactions.

⑧ Click the window's **Close (X)** button to close the Scheduled Transaction List.

⚠ **WARNING**
For payments scheduled on the actual bill due date, increase the **Record This Many Days In Advance** setting to at least seven. Now, you can print and mail the check a week before, avoiding a late payment.

End Task

Task 6: Recalling a Scheduled Transaction

Using Your Scheduled Transaction

When you start Quicken, upcoming scheduled transactions are listed on the My Finances Center. You should get in the habit of checking this list to make sure you enter any scheduled transaction that you didn't tell Quicken to enter automatically. You use the Scheduled Transaction List to select and enter the next instance of the scheduled transaction into the register. Then you can view or work with the transaction in the register.

✓ **Entered Automatically**
Be sure to print checks for scheduled transactions that Quicken enters automatically.

✓ **More Memory Help**
You also can use the *Reminders* and *Billminder* features to help you remember scheduled transactions. See Tasks 7 and 8 to learn how to turn on and use these features.

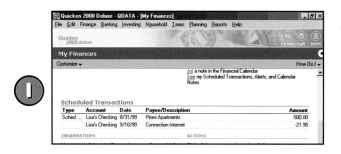

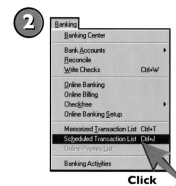

Click

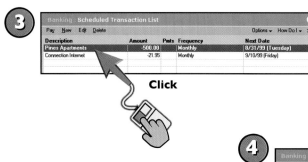

Click

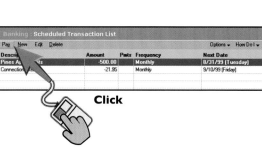

Click

① When you start Quicken, scroll down to check for due transactions in the Scheduled Transaction List on the My Finance Center.

② Choose **Banking, Scheduled Transaction List (Ctrl+J)**.

③ Click the scheduled transaction you want to use.

④ Click the **Pay** button on the Scheduled Transaction List window toolbar.

Next Step ▶

⑤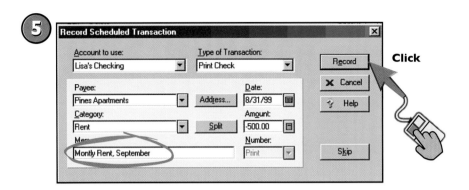

Click

Finishing the Job

Quicken can help you remember to enter a scheduled transaction, but it doesn't remind you to print the checks for these transactions. This burden falls on your shoulders. Refer to Part 1, Task 19, for a refresher on how to print checks you've set up to print.

⑥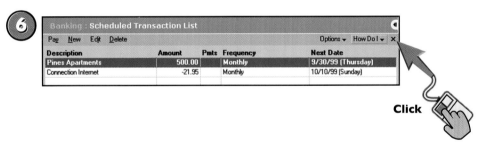

Click

✅ **Scheduled Transaction Changes**
Task 9 explains how to change or delete a scheduled transaction.

✅ **Next, Please**
After you "pay" or enter a particular scheduled transaction, Quicken updates the Scheduled Transaction List with the date for the next instance of that transaction.

⑤ Adjust any of the transaction entries as needed and click **Record**.

⑥ After repeating steps 3–5 to enter other scheduled transactions, click the **Close (X)** button.

End Task

Task 7: Using Reminders

Seeing Transaction Reminders When You Start Quicken

When you turn on the *Reminders* feature, it appears when you start Quicken to list upcoming scheduled transactions. By default, the Reminders feature adds the next instance of a scheduled transaction to the list at least seven days before the transaction is due.

✓ Alert! Alert!
You also can create an *Alert* to warn you of a particular situation. Alerts appear in the Reminders window and the My Finances Center.

✓ More Days
You can control how many days in advance you want the Reminders window to list scheduled transactions. Click the **Options** button, choose **Reminders,** and click **Days Shown.** Change the **Days in Advance** entry and click **OK.**

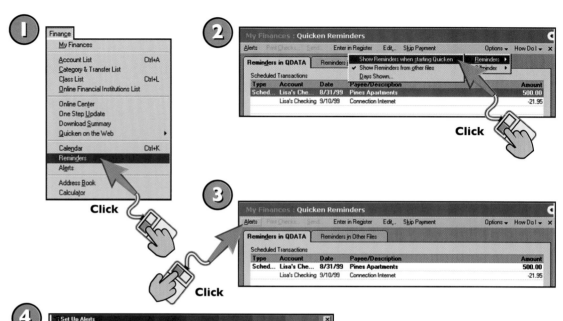

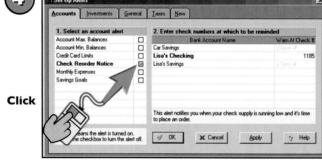

① Choose **Finance**, **Reminders**.

② Click **Options** on the Quicken Reminders toolbar, point to **Reminders**, and click **Show Reminders When Starting Quicken**.

③ Click the **Alerts** button on the toolbar.

④ Check an Alert type, enter the Alert value, and then click **OK**.

Next Step

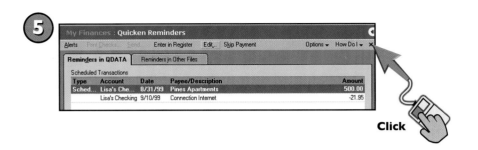

5

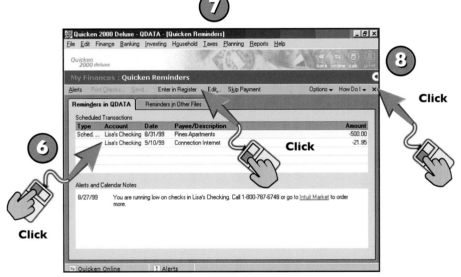

6 **7** **8**

Using the Reminder

When the Reminders appear, you need to select a reminder and tell Quicken to enter a transaction for it in the register. This process will seem familiar to you, because it resembles the process for entering a scheduled transaction. After you enter the transaction, be sure to go to the register and print a check for it, if needed.

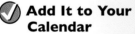 **Add It to Your Calendar**
Quicken Deluxe 2000 offers a new feature called the Financial Calendar that you can use to schedule upcoming bills. Choose **Finance, Financial Calendar** to display the calendar, and then drag a memorized transaction from the list at the right onto the desired date.

5 Click the **Close (X)** button on the Quicken Reminders window to close it.

6 When you restart Quicken later, click the scheduled transaction you want to enter into the register.

7 Click **Enter in Register** on the toolbar to enter the transaction in the register.

8 Click the **Close (X)** button on the Quicken Reminders Window to close it.

Task 8: Using Billminder

Start Here

Seeing Transaction Reminders When You Start Windows

The *Billminder* feature appears when you start Windows (not Quicken) to list reminders of upcoming scheduled transactions, checks you need to print, and more. You should take advantage of this feature if you use Quicken infrequently or have Quicken automatically enter scheduled transactions. Paying attention to Billminder almost guarantees that you won't miss any payments. The Billminder feature doesn't work by default; you have to turn it on to get it started.

✓ **Billminder to Reminders**

If you have Reminders turned on, starting Quicken from the Quicken Billminder window takes you directly to the Quicken Reminders window, so you can skip step 5.

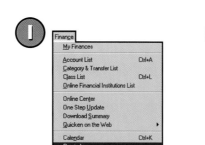

Click

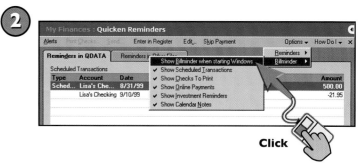

Click

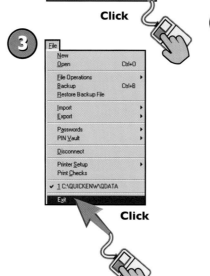

Click

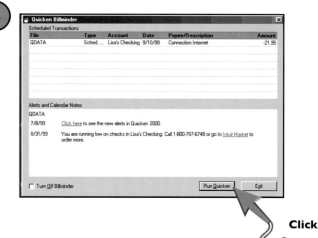

Click

 Choose **Finance**, **Reminders**.

 Click **Options** on the Quicken Reminders window toolbar, point to **Billminder**, and click **Show Billminder When Starting Windows**.

 After you finish your work, choose **File**, **Exit** to exit Quicken.

 If the Quicken Billminder window appears when you start Windows, click **Run Quicken**.

Next Step

Using the Billminder

While it's turned on, Billminder loads automatically each time you start Windows. If it contains any scheduled transaction reminders or Alerts to pass along, the Quicken Billminder window opens. You can then start Quicken, display the Reminders window or Scheduled Transaction List, and enter the selected transaction.

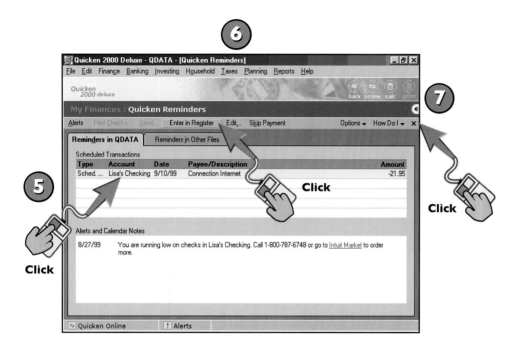

5 Click the scheduled transaction you want to enter into the register.

6 Click **Enter in Register** on the toolbar to enter the transaction in the register.

7 Click the **Close (X)** button on the Quicken Reminders window to close it.

✅ **On and Off**
The same commands that you use to turn on Reminders and Billminder also toggle Reminders and Billminder off again.

✅ **No More Reminders**
To turn Billminder off, check **Turn Off Billminder** in the Billminder window.

Task 9: Editing or Deleting a Scheduled Transaction

Updating Scheduled Transactions

As with other information you capture with your computer, the information in the Scheduled Transaction List doesn't stay current forever. For example, say you move from one apartment to another. In such a case, you need to change the scheduled transaction for your rent payment to use another Payee (the new landlord) and Amount (usually always more than you used to pay). Of course, both the Reminders list and Billminder adjust to reflect your changes.

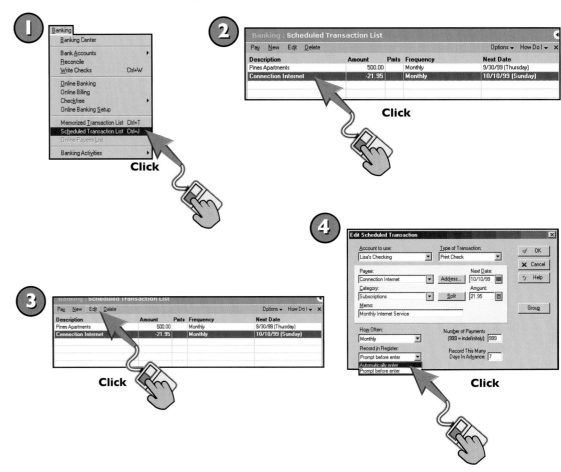

Click

Click

Click

Click

① Choose **Banking**, **Scheduled Transaction List** (**Ctrl+J**).

② Click the scheduled transaction you want to edit.

③ Click the **Edit** button on the Scheduled Transaction List window toolbar.

④ Make any changes needed to the transaction information and click **OK**.

Next Step

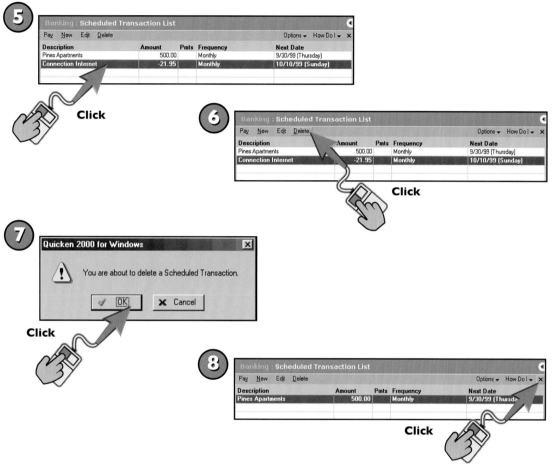

Some scheduled transactions become obsolete. Suppose you buy a house and ditch your apartment. You then need to create a scheduled transaction for entering your mortgage payment, which you've already learned, and delete the unneeded scheduled transaction.

---

5 To delete a scheduled transaction, click the scheduled transaction you want to delete.

6 Click the **Delete** button on the Scheduled Transaction List window toolbar.

7 Click **OK** to confirm the deletion.

8 Click the **Close (X)** button on the Scheduled Transaction List window to close it.

 WARNING
After you delete a scheduled transaction, you can't undo the deletion, so choose wisely.

Task 10: Grouping Transactions

Creating a Transaction Group

The Reminders window saves time, but it lets you enter (pay) only one transaction at a time. To gain the ability to enter multiple transactions at once, you need to create a *transaction group* in the Scheduled Transaction List. You save a list of memorized transactions under a group name, specifying how often Quicken should schedule all of the transactions in the group. Quicken adds the group to the list of Reminders.

✅ **Timing the Group**
Transaction groups should hold only similarly timed bills—within the same week, for instance. Your **Next Date** schedules the group's first due date.

✅ **Investments**
To group investment transactions, you need to click **Investment** under Group Type.

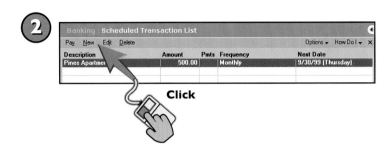

Click

Click

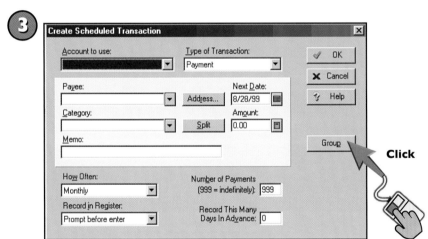

Click

① Choose **Banking**, **Scheduled Transaction List** (**Ctrl+J**).

② Click the **New** button on the Scheduled Transaction List window toolbar.

③ Click the **Group** button in the Create Scheduled Transaction dialog box.

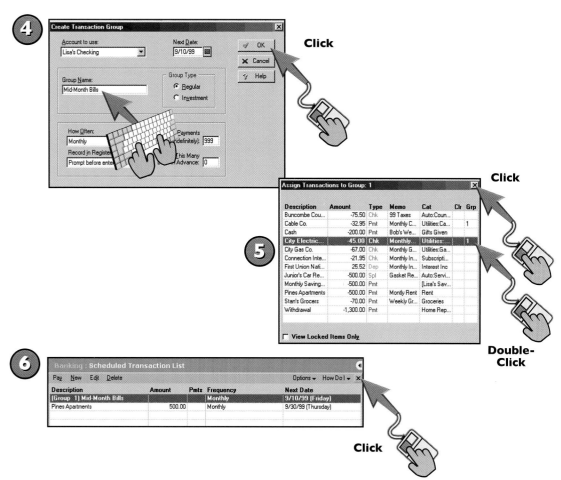

Click

Click

Double-Click

Click

Identifying Transactions to Group

You can group only memorized transactions. If a transaction you want to add to the group doesn't appear in the list, you'll need to memorize the transaction and then add it to the group later. See Task 12 to learn how to change a transaction group.

✓ By the Numbers

Quicken numbers each new transaction group you create, so the number in the Grp column of the Assign Transactions To window tells you what group a transaction falls into.

✓ Mark, Unmark

In the Assign Transactions To Group window, double-clicking the group number in the Grp column for a transaction removes the number, thus removing the transaction from the group.

(4) Enter a **Group Name** and specify all of the other information for the group. Click **OK**.

(5) In the Assign Transactions to Group window, double-click the **Grp** column for each transaction (row) you want to add to the transaction group, and then click the **Close** (**X**) button.

(6) Click the **Close** (**X**) button on the Scheduled Transaction List window to close it.

Task 11: Using the Transaction Group

Entering the Grouped Transactions

After you've added a transaction group to the Scheduled Transaction List, Quicken treats the transaction group just like any other scheduled transaction. You can "pay" the transaction from the Scheduled Transaction List. When you have Reminders or Billminder turned on (see Tasks 7 and 8), Quicken reminds you when you need to enter the group. Entering the group enters a copy in the register of each of the transactions the group holds. This task shows how it looks to use the group from the Reminders list.

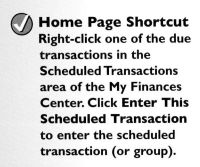

Home Page Shortcut
Right-click one of the due transactions in the Scheduled Transactions area of the My Finances Center. Click **Enter This Scheduled Transaction** to enter the scheduled transaction (or group).

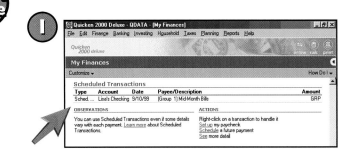

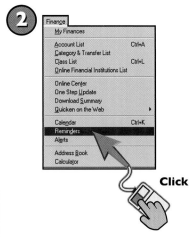

Click

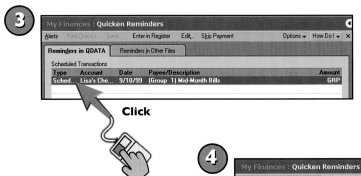

Click

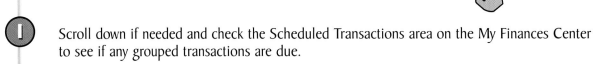

Click

(1) Scroll down if needed and check the Scheduled Transactions area on the My Finances Center to see if any grouped transactions are due.

(2) If a group is due to be paid, choose **Finance**, **Reminders**.

(3) Click the transaction group in the list of reminders, if needed.

(4) Click the **Enter in Register** button on the Scheduled Transaction List window toolbar.

Next Step

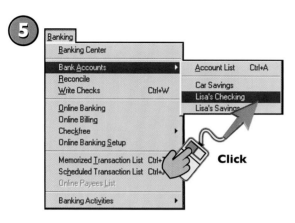

It's a good idea to check the scheduled transactions in the register and to make any needed changes, particularly if not all of the bills use the same amount. In addition, you need to remember to print the checks for the transactions, if needed.

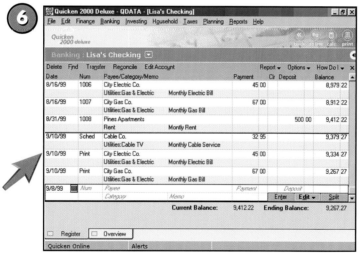

Choose **Banking**, **Bank Accounts**, and then click the name of the account you want to view.

Review your transactions and edit them or print checks as needed.

 Back and Forward
Each of the Quicken window title bars includes left arrow (Back) and right arrow (Forward) buttons. You can click these buttons to move between open Quicken windows.

Task 12: Editing a Transaction Group

Making Changes to Your Group

Just as individual scheduled transactions can become outdated, a transaction group might need changes from time to time to remain as useful as possible. You can change the general description and scheduling information you initially specified for the group, such as the Group Name and the Next Date (scheduled transaction date).

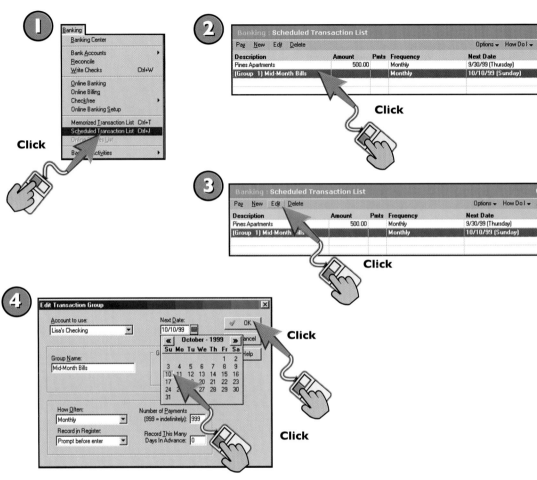

Start Here

Click

Click

Click

Click

Click

Click

1. Choose **Banking, Scheduled Transaction List (Ctrl+J)**.

2. Click the transaction group to change, if needed.

3. Click the **Edit** button on the Scheduled Transaction List window toolbar.

4. Change the date, group, and other information as needed and click **OK**.

Next Step

Click

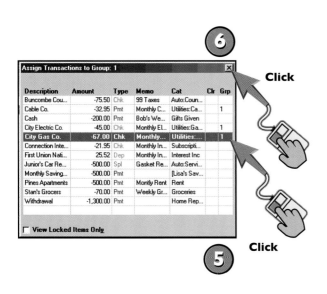

Click

Click

Changing and Removing Transactions

Editing a transaction group also gives you the opportunity to adjust which transactions the group includes. For example, you might need to remove an outdated transaction from the group, or add a transaction the group didn't previously include.

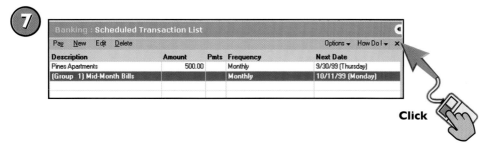

Click

5 In the Assign Transactions to Group window, double-click the **Grp** column for each transaction (row) to remove it from or add it to the transaction group.

6 Click the **Close (X)** button to close the Assign Transactions to Group window.

7 Click the **Close (X)** button on the Scheduled Transaction List window to close it.

End Task

Task 13: Printing the Scheduled Transaction List

Getting a Transaction List to Go

If you print a list of your scheduled transactions, you can place it in a noticeable location, such as on the fridge, in your schedule book, right in your paper checkbook. You might want to do this if you use the computer infrequently and sometimes forget to fire up Quicken and pay your bills. If Quicken enters the transactions automatically for you but you don't print out the checks, refer to the list to hand-write checks.

⊘ WARNING

You must display the Scheduled Transaction List before you try to print it. If you're displaying an account register instead, Quicken prints the account register.

✓ Print It

If you don't want to preview the list printout, just click **OK** rather than **Preview** (step 4) and skip the rest of the steps.

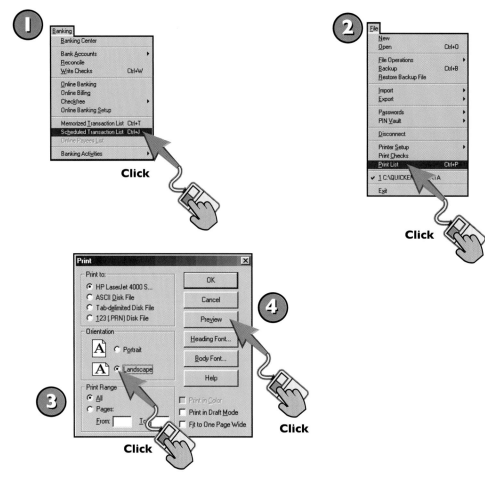

Start Here

Click

Click

Click

Click

① Choose **Banking**, **Scheduled Transaction List** (**Ctrl+J**).

② Choose **File**, **Print List** (**Ctrl+P**).

③ Specify the settings you want to use for printing (for example, choose **Landscape**).

④ Click the **Preview** button.

Next Step

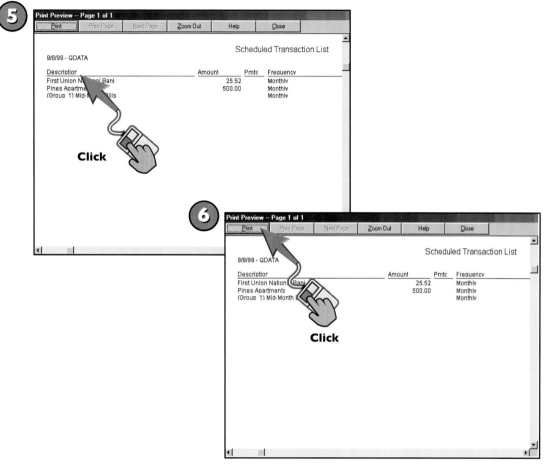

Getting a Preview

When you're printing a list or report (but not checks), the Print dialog box offers a Preview button. You can click the **Preview** button to display a preview of how the printout will look. After you review the preview, you can return to the Print dialog box or even the report itself to make adjustments before you finish the print job.

5 Click any part of the preview to zoom in (or back out).

6 Click **Print** to send the list to the printer.

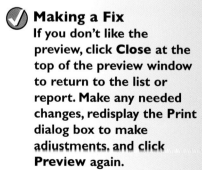 **Making a Fix**
If you don't like the preview, click **Close** at the top of the preview window to return to the list or report. Make any needed changes, redisplay the Print dialog box to make adjustments, and click **Preview** again.

Task 14: Using Paycheck Setup

Tracking Your Payroll Taxes

If you don't plan to use Quicken to track information for tax time, you can simply enter a transaction for the net pay amount you receive for each paycheck. If you want Quicken to prepare tax information for you, it needs to know each tax amount withheld from each paycheck. Run Paycheck Setup to tell Quicken how to enter each pay and tax component of your paycheck at pay time.

✓ **Seen It Before?**
Click **New** to create a new paycheck or **Edit** to change an existing one. The steps are different from the ones shown here if you have already done Paycheck Setup.

✓ **Going Back**
You can click the **Back** button while using Paycheck Setup to return to a previous dialog box and change your entries or choices.

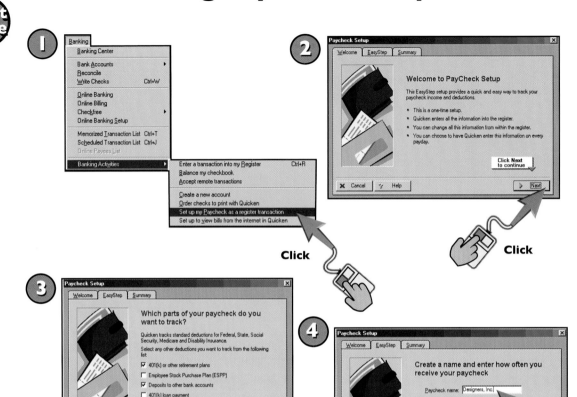

Start Here

Click

Click

Click

① Choose **Banking**, **Banking Activities**, **Set Up My Paycheck as a Register Transaction**.

② Review the information in the first dialog box, and then click **Next**.

③ Click to remove the check marks beside items you don't want to track, and then click **Next**.

④ Enter a **Paycheck Name** and specify how often you're paid. Click **Next**.

Next Step

Click

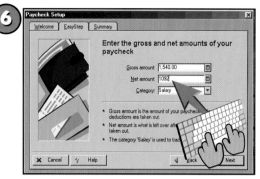

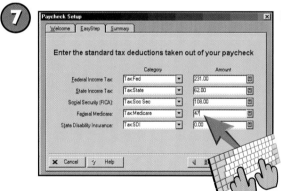

Click

Getting It Right

Have your most recent paycheck on hand and use its date as the Date of This Paycheck entry. Also refer to the recent paycheck for accurate pay and tax information. If you opt in step 8 to set up the paycheck as a Scheduled Transaction, Quicken enters the transaction for you. You don't need a reminder, and you can edit the transaction entry in the register, if needed. You also can select the paycheck transaction in the Scheduled Transaction List and click the Edit button to start Paycheck Setup and make changes to the transaction.

✅ **Extra Steps**
Depending on your selections from step 3, Paycheck Setup might present even more steps than are covered here. Quicken asks you all of the questions you need to answer to set up the paycheck correctly.

5 From your most current paycheck, specify the date of the paycheck and the account in which you want your paychecks deposited. Click **Next**.

6 Enter the **Gross Amount** and **Net Amount** from your recent paycheck. Change the **Category**, if needed, and then click **Next**.

7 Enter bonuses or other pay and click **Next**. Enter paycheck deductions and click **Next**. Enter additional taxes and deductions and click **Next**.

8 Click **Yes** and then **Next** to set up your paycheck as a scheduled transaction. Review the summary, and click **Done**.

Account Balancing and Reporting

When you capture the right information about your personal finances, you acquire the power to identify your strong and weak points. You can make better decisions about what to do with your money and feel pleased with the progress you've already made. This part teaches you how to reconcile an account's balance to ensure you have the right information and how to generate a report that summarizes information in an account.

Tasks

Task 1: Starting the Reconciliation Process

Getting Started with Your Paper Statement

When you balance a paper checkbook, you *reconcile* your check register to make sure the balance matches the balance on the statement from your bank. Similarly, each time you receive a paper statement for a bank, credit card, or other account, you need to reconcile the corresponding Quicken account with the statement. Start by entering information from your paper statement into Quicken.

✓ Online Reconciliation
Online banking makes it easier to enter and reconcile your account. See the first three tasks in Part 6.

✓ Service Charges and Interest
Enter any monthly service charge for your account during this first reconciliation stage, but not ATM fees or bounced check charges. Also, enter any interest earned at this time.

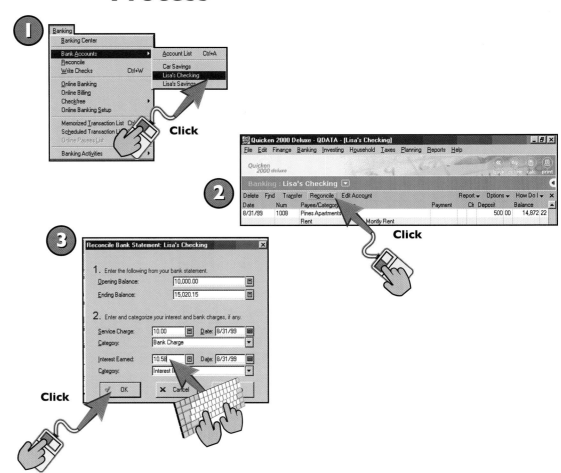

① Choose **Banking**, **Bank Accounts**, and then click the name of the account to reconcile.

② Click the **Reconcile** button on the register window toolbar.

③ In the Reconcile Bank Statement dialog box, fill in information from your paper statement, click **OK**, and move on to the next task.

Task 2: Clearing a Transaction

Start Here

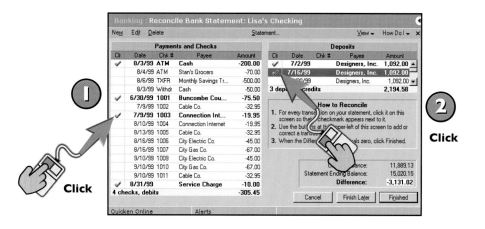

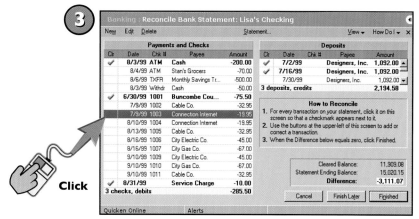

1 In the Payments and Checks list, click in the **Clr** column to check each cleared transaction.

2 In the Deposits list, click in the **Clr** column to check each cleared transaction.

3 In either list, click a transaction's check mark in the **Clr** column to remove the check mark from a transaction that has not cleared.

Marking Off Transactions from Your Paper Statement

When your financial institution executes a transaction (pays a check or deposits interest), that transaction has *cleared*. Correspondingly, you must mark these cleared transactions from your paper statement as cleared in Quicken. As you clear transactions, the Difference amount in the lower-right corner of the Reconcile (Account) Statement window decreases. If you don't get to 0 just by clearing transactions, use the techniques covered in Tasks 3–5 to reduce it to 0.

✅ **Statement Changes**
If you realize you made an error when entering information from your statement in the last task, click the **Statement** button on the toolbar, make the needed changes, and click **OK**.

Task 3: Adjusting a Transaction

Adjusting Transactions to Match Your Paper Statement

We have to scrutinize paper and Quicken transactions to verify consistency. For example, even though your paycheck might always be about the same amount, occasionally your employer might need to adjust your pay by a few cents or a few dollars to ensure you're paid the right total for the year. You can adjust a Quicken transaction from the Reconcile (Account) Statement window so its dollar value matches the amount on the paper statement.

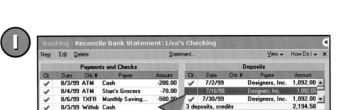

Click

Click

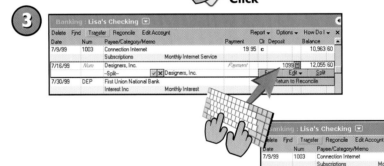

Click

✓ **Don't Let It Be Accurate** records keep you out of trouble down the line, so it's important to fix transaction amounts. You might discover that your employer underpaid you or the bank overcharged you, and you can get some money back.

① In the Payments and Checks or Deposits list, click the transaction you want to adjust.

② Click the **Edit** button on the Reconcile (Account) Statement window toolbar.

③ In the register, edit the transaction **Payment** or **Deposit** amount and any other information, as needed.

④ Click the **Enter** button below the transaction.

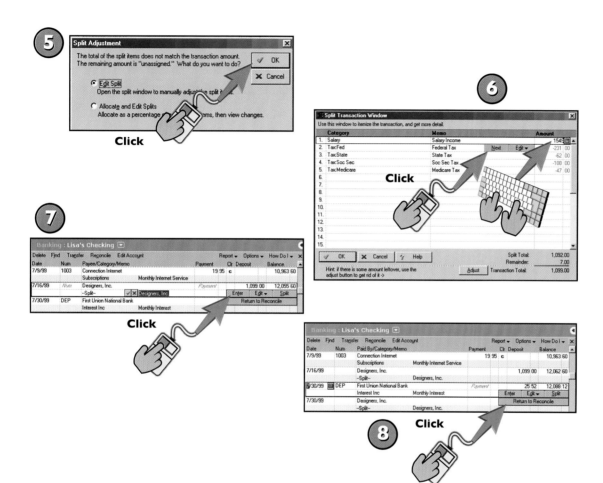

Finishing the Adjustment

When you start the reconciliation process and select (click) a transaction to adjust, Quicken removes the check mark from the Clr column for that transaction if you previously marked it as cleared. When you finish these steps and return to the Reconcile (Account) Statement window, be sure to click the Clr column for the transaction to re-mark it.

✅ **Percentage, Please**
To automatically update the category amounts for an adjusted split transaction, click the **Allocate and Edit Splits** option button before clicking **OK** in step 6.

✅ **Remainder**
The Remainder amount at tells you the total you have to add to or remove from the category amounts.

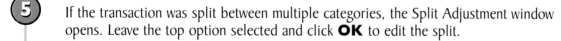

(5) If the transaction was split between multiple categories, the Split Adjustment window opens. Leave the top option selected and click **OK** to edit the split.

(6) Edit amounts as needed, click **Next** to accept each change, and then click **OK**.

(7) Click **Enter** below the transaction to accept changes.

(8) Click **Return to Reconcile**. Click the **Clr** column for the transaction to clear it, if needed.

End Task

Task 4: Entering a Missing Transaction

Adding Transactions to Match Your Paper Statement

Suppose you've marked all of the cleared transactions that show up in the Reconcile (Account) Statement window, and you've adjusted a couple of transactions, but you still have a difference greater than 0 in the lower-right corner of the Reconcile (Account) Statement window. At this point, you need to check for transactions on your paper account statement for which you haven't entered a corresponding transaction in Quicken. Examples include charges for insufficient funds (bounced check) and ATM use. Follow along now to learn how to enter such a transaction.

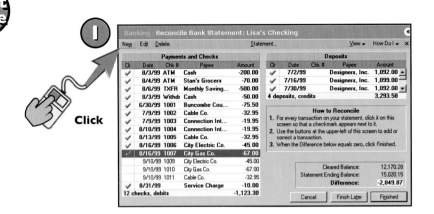

Click

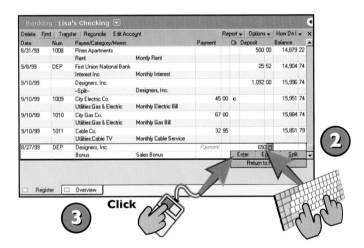

Click

① Click the **New** button on the Reconcile (Account) Statement window toolbar.

② In the register, enter all of the transaction information as usual.

③ Click the **Enter** button below the transaction.

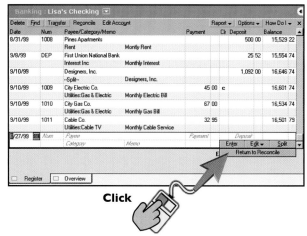

Click

Deleting a Transaction While Reconciling

Of course, correcting an extra transaction can work out in your favor, too! For example, you could enter some type of transaction fee and then find that the fee doesn't show up on your statement. To remove any extra transaction while reconciling, click the transaction in the Reconcile (Account) Statement window and then click **Delete** on the window toolbar. Click **Yes** to confirm the deletion.

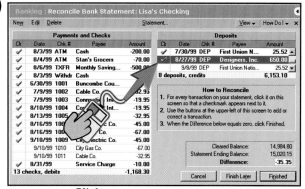

Click

Click **Return to Reconcile**.

Click the **Clr** column for the transaction to clear it.

Task 5: Finishing and Printing the Reconciliation

Taking Your Last Reconciliation Steps

If you've followed along so far, you've marked all cleared transactions, adjusted transactions, and entered missing transactions. If the difference amount in the lower right corner of the Reconcile (Account) Statement window still isn't 0, it's okay. As you finish the reconciliation process, Quicken will enter a balance adjustment transaction for you to bring everything into synch. If your account already balances, this process will go even faster for you.

✓ Later, Gator

If you decide at any time that you don't have time to finish the reconciliation process, click the **Finish Later** button. When you later have time to restart reconciliation, the transactions you marked as cleared remain marked.

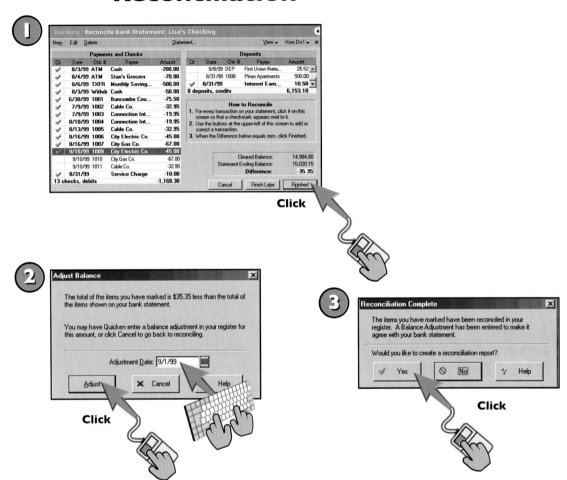

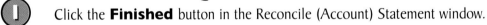

① Click the **Finished** button in the Reconcile (Account) Statement window.

② If an Adjust Balance window appears, specify an **Adjustment Date** and then click **Adjust**.

③ Click **Yes** to have Quicken generate a report about the reconciliation activity.

Next Step

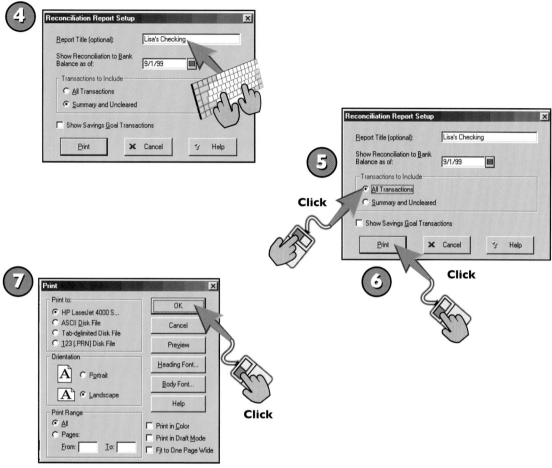

Printing a Reconciliation Report

You could click **No** in step 3 to skip printing a reconciliation report. If you didn't initially print a reconciliation report but later decide to do so, display the register for the reconciled account, choose **Reports, Banking, Reconciliation,** and pick up with the steps on this page.

✅ **Gimme an R**
When you return to the register after reconciling an account, each cleared and reconciled transaction displays an **R** in the **Clr** column.

✅ **Uncleared Transactions**
The reconciliation report also identifies transactions that haven't cleared, so you can check for them when you receive your next account statement.

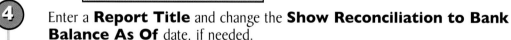

④ Enter a **Report Title** and change the **Show Reconciliation to Bank Balance As Of** date, if needed.

⑤ To print all reconciled transactions, select the **All Transactions** option, if it isn't selected.

⑥ Click **Print**.

⑦ Make any selections you want from the Print dialog box and click **OK** to print the report.

Task 6: Viewing a Report

Building a Report in the Reports and Graphs Center

Quicken Deluxe 2000 offers a new way to access reports and graphs: The Reports and Graphs Center. This Center enables you to find the answer to a particular question with regard to your finances. After you make just a few quick selections, Quicken displays the report for you onscreen so you can adjust or print it.

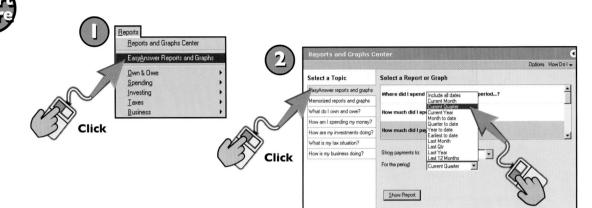

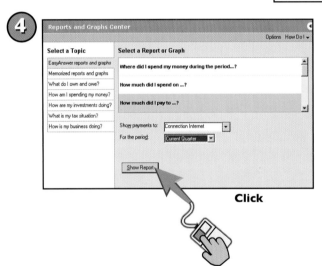

✓ **To the Reports and Graphs**

You also use the Reports and Graphs Center command on the Reports menu or can click the Reports and Graphs QuickTab to display the Reports and Graphs Center.

1. Choose **Reports, EasyAnswer Reports and Graphs**.

2. Click the question you want to answer or the **EasyAnswer Reports and Graphs** choice in the list at the left.

3. Make your selections from the drop-down list or lists that appear at the right.

4. Click **Show Report** to display the report.

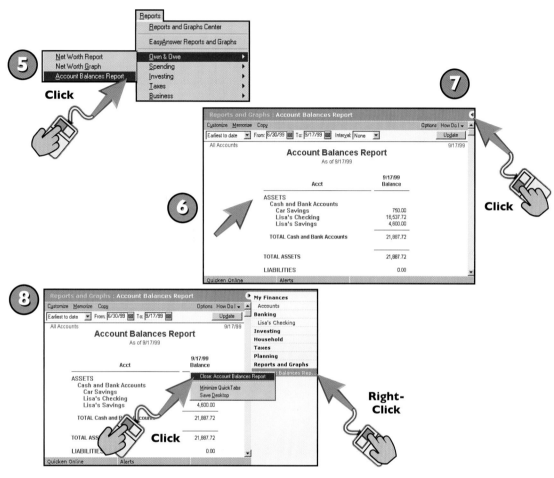

Choosing a Report by Category

To view and select one of the reports that applies to a particular type of activity or one of the reports that has to do with spending or taxes, you can use another technique to display the report you need. The Reports menu lists different categories of reports. Select a report category and then select the report to display.

⑤ Open the **Reports** menu and point to a category to display its submenu; click the report you want.

⑥ Review your report information.

⑦ Click the handle for the QuickTabs column to display the QuickTabs if needed.

⑧ Right-click the QuickTab for the report, then click **Close: (Report Name)**.

Task 7: Modifying a Report

Customizing Your Report

Although Quicken offers a number of reports, you might not find a report that fits your needs—exactly. If you find a report that's close to what you want, you can modify the report so it uses the format and displays the information you need.

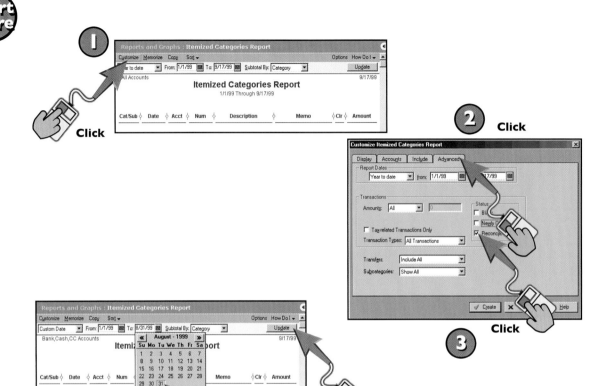

✓ Zoom It
If a report lists a transaction or summary line you want to see more information about, point to it. When you see the zoom pointer (z), click. Quicken jumps to the transaction in the register or displays more details.

✓ Drag a Column
If your report contains blue column headings with vertical hash marks, you can drag a hash mark to change the column width.

(1) Click the **Customize** button on the report window toolbar.

(2) Click a tab to display its options.

(3) Change the settings you want and click **Create**.

(4) You also can change one of the settings below the toolbar and click **Update**.

Click

Memorizing a Report and Using It Later

You've now peeked at the report settings, so you've seen how many of them Quicken offers. You might have to make several changes and selections to set up a report so it's the way you want it. Rather than reinventing the wheel later, you can memorize your report and recall the *memorized report* to view it again.

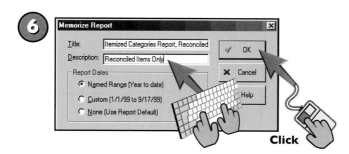

Click

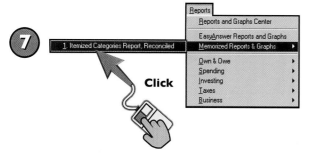

Click

---

5 Click the **Memorize** button on the report window toolbar.

6 Specify a title and dates for the report, a description (optional), and an icon. Click **OK**.

7 Choose **Reports**, **Memorized Reports & Graphs**, and then click the name of the memorized report to open on the submenu.

✅ **Missing Command?**
The Memorized Reports & Graphs command doesn't appear on the Reports menu until after you memorize your first report.

PART 3

Task 8: Printing a Report

Setting Up Your Report for Printing

You can print out a report after you display it for record-keeping purposes. Even though Quicken keeps your transactions electronically, you might sometimes need a hard copy, such as if you need to share records with a bank or lender. Before you print, you can select options that apply to report printing in Quicken.

Start Here

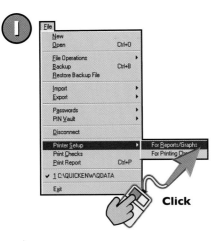
Click

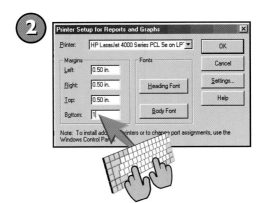

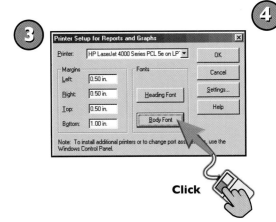
Click

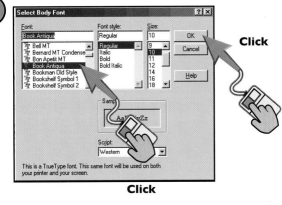
Click **Click**

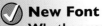
New Font

Whether you click the Heading Font or Body Font button in the Printer Setup for Reports and Graphs dialog box, the choices in the resulting dialog box are the same. The difference is where Quicken applies your choices.

① Choose **File**, **Printer Setup**, **For Reports/Graphs**.

② Make a new entry, if needed, for any of the settings in the **Margins** area.

③ If needed, click either the **Heading Font** or **Body Font** button.

④ Make your **Font**, **Font Style**, and **Size** choices. Click **OK** and then **OK** again.

Next Step

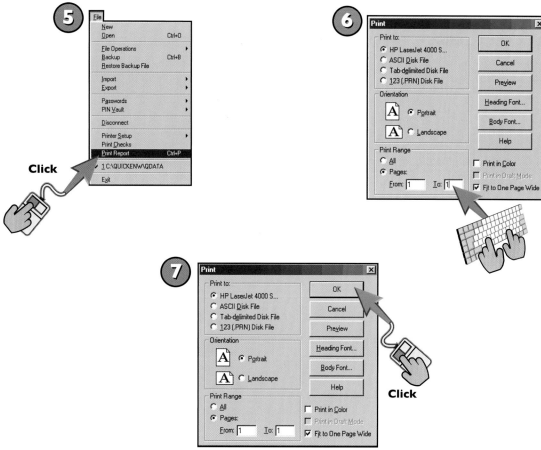

Finishing the Print Job

After you've chosen your printout settings for a report, you can finish the print job. Keep in mind that the report you want to print must be displayed in Quicken before you can print it. Then you can proceed as described on this page to print.

Choose **File**, **Print Report** (**Ctrl+P**).

Adjust any Print dialog box settings as needed.

Click **OK** to print the report.

✓ **And Graphs, Too**
The settings you select for your report printing also apply to printouts of graphs you display in Quicken. See Task 9 to learn how to display and print a graph.

✓ **Preview It**
In Part 2, Task 13, you learned how to use the Preview button in the Print dialog box. You can use the same technique to preview a report printout.

Task 9: Displaying and Adjusting a Graph

Charting Your Results

If you're not a numbers person, a report might not fit the bill for you. In such a case, you can display a graph of your account information. Graphs give you a visual representation of how category totals (or other significant account summary information) stack up against each other. This task shows you how to select the graph you want from using the Reports and Graphs Center.

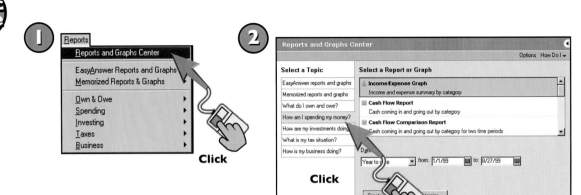

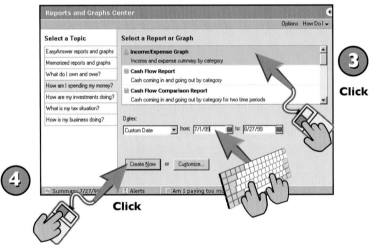

1. Choose **Reports**, **Reports and Graphs Center**.

2. Click the question you want to answer or the **EasyAnswer Reports and Graphs** choice in the list at the left.

3. Choose a graph from the top list at the right, and then adjust the graph using the applicable drop-down lists.

4. Click **Create Now** to display the graph.

Next Step

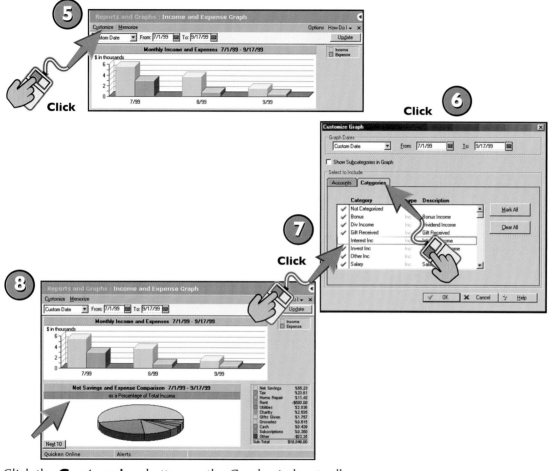

Adjusting Your Graph

As with a report, a default graph you display might need a bit of tweaking to fit your needs. If the graph shows too much data, you might have difficulty picking out the information you need. If it shows too little, it can be virtually meaningless. You can adjust or customize a graph you display in Quicken so it better represents your account information.

Click the **Customize** button on the Graph window toolbar.

Click a tab to display its options.

Change the settings you want and click **OK**.

Double-check that the graph now shows the information you need, and repeat steps 5–7 if needed.

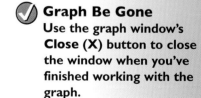

Graph Be Gone
Use the graph window's **Close (X)** button to close the window when you've finished working with the graph.

Task 10: Memorizing and Printing a Graph

Saving the Graph Settings

As with a report, you don't want to specify all of your graph settings more than once. If your intent is to save time, you'll save even more time if you memorize (save) a graph so you can easily recall it later.

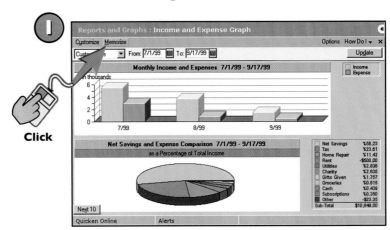

Click

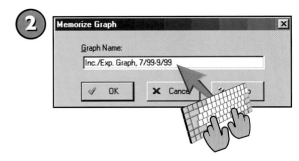

 Good Graph Name
When you memorize a report or graph, I suggest using the word "report" or "graph" in the name, as appropriate. This ensures you'll be able to recall the correct memorized item.

1 Click the **Memorize** button on the Graph window toolbar.

2 Specify a **Graph Name**.

Printing Your Graph

Again, you might want to print a graph to have a record of it. The steps you use to print a graph greatly resemble the steps for printing a report. In fact, if you've set up a corresponding graph and report, having a printout of each can provide an impressive package to show a loan officer or banker if you're trying to secure financing or a personal financial planner if you're looking for financial guidance.

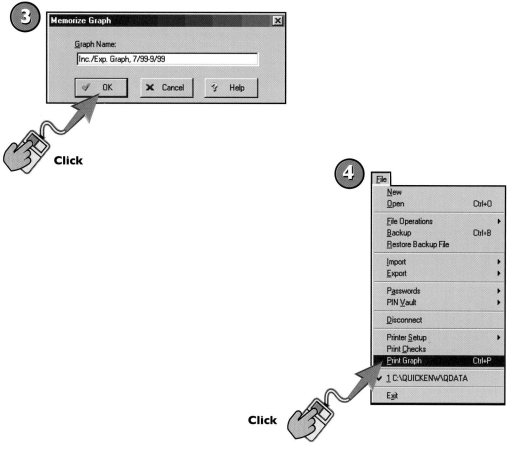

Click

Click

③ Click **OK**.

④ Choose **File**, **Print Graph** (**Ctrl+P**) to send the graph to the printer.

✅ **Recall Your Graph**
To redisplay a graph you've memorized, choose **Reports, Memorized Reports & Graphs**. In the submenu, click the graph to display and then click **Use** on the toolbar.

Tracking Your Investments and Loans

Recent tax law changes and other factors have contributed to booms in both the investment and home markets. People invest in mutual funds, stocks, and bonds to help increase personal wealth. Concurrently, favorable interest rates help folks feel comfortable enough to take on some debt, so they buy a larger house or car or charge a little bit more on a credit card. Keeping investment inflows and interest outflows in balance requires careful management, and Quicken offers tools you can use.

Tasks

Task 1: Creating an Investment Account

Tracking Multiple Investments

In Quicken, you create an *investment account* for each brokerage statement you receive. You can use it to track changes to the share price or value of each investment you add to the account. The investment account also handles the special types of transactions you make with securities, such as stock splits and fluctuations in value.

✓ Investment Versus Asset

Quicken offers a variety of investment accounts. For certain types of investments, such as real estate, you might need to create an *asset account* instead. Choose **Help, Index.** Type invest, and double-click **Setting Up** under Investment Accounts to learn more about the various types of investment accounts.

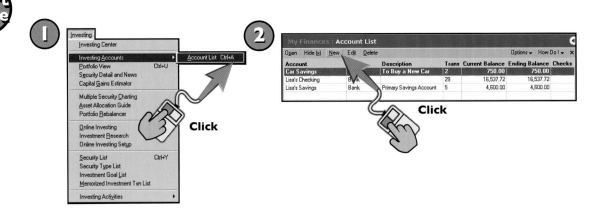

Click

Click

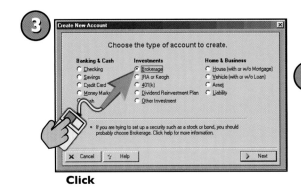

Click

Start Here

1. Choose **Investing**, **Investing Accounts**, **Account List** (**Ctrl+A**) to display the Account List.

2. Click the **New** button on the Account List window toolbar.

3. In the Create New Account window, click the appropriate option button under **Investments**, and then click **Next**.

4. Specify an **Account Name**, **Description**, and **Financial Institution**, and click **Next**. Leave **No** selected and click **Next**.

Next Step

Click

Finishing the Account

After you've entered the account information, Quicken prompts you to enter the investments the account holds (stocks or mutual funds, for example). To learn how to enter an investment, pick up with step 3 of Task 2.

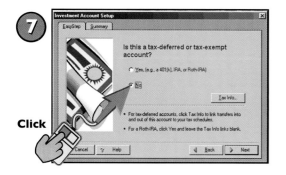

Click

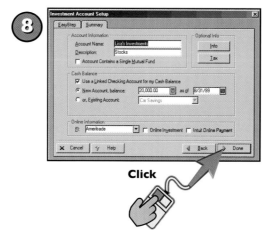

Click

✔ **Account Cash**
If your investment account holds cash in addition to securities, you need to set up a linked checking account. As the opening balance, enter the amount of cash plus the opening value for all securities, because Quicken deducts the initial share "purchase" from the linked checking account for each security. If you're planning to enter historical data for the account (all purchases, sales, and so on), also specify an **As Of** date that corresponds with the date when you opened the Investment account.

⑤ If you need to set up an associated checking account, click **Yes** and then **Next** to create a linked checking account. Enter the **Balance** amount and **As Of** date.

⑥ Click an option to describe the account's contents and then click **Next**.

⑦ Click an option to specify whether the account is tax deferred and then click **Next**.

⑧ Verify and correct the account information and then click **Done** to finish. When prompted to set up securities, click **Next** and then skip to step 3 of the next task.

Defining the Account's Investments

In each Quicken investment account, you have to specify what investments the account holds—which stocks, mutual funds, and bonds. When you add the investment, you specify the number of shares, your purchase price, and any fees or commissions involved. As noted in the previous task, when you set up the account, Quicken prompts you to add investments. Any time you purchase a new investment, such as buying a stock not previously held in the account, you need to add that new investment to the investment account as described here.

✓ **Display the Account**
To open an investment account, choose **Investing, Investing Accounts,** and then click the investment account you'd like to open in the submenu.

Task 2: Adding an Investment

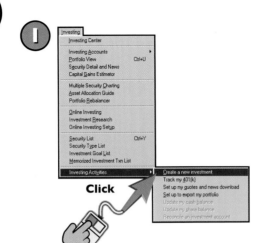

Click

Click

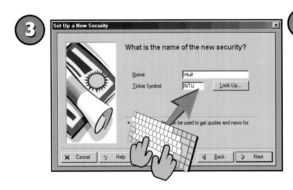

Click

① Choose **Investing**, **Investing Activities**, **Create a New Investment**.

② Leave **I Want To Set Up a New Security in an Existing Account** selected, and click **OK**. Click **Next**.

③ Select the security type and click **Next**. Then enter its name and ticker symbol. Click **Next**.

④ Specify asset class and goal information, and then click **Next**.

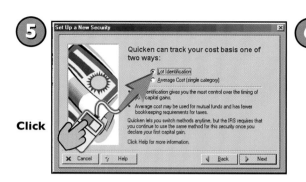

Click

Click

Determining How Far Back to Track

Note that in step 6 you can also start tracking the stock from the end of the prior year or from its actual purchase date. You should choose one of these options to enable you to track tax information for the investment for the current year or for all years since the purchase. For the most accurate record, select the bottom option button and give the purchase date. Then you'll need to enter all transactions made since the stock purchase—every purchase, sale, dividend, and so on—into the account register.

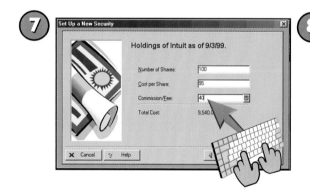

Click

✅ **On What Basis?**
In step 5 you select the cost basis for your investment. If you've previously used a particular basis for that investment, you might be required to stick with the same basis.

---

5 Select a cost basis method and click **Next**.

6 Leave **Today** selected (if the current date is your purchase date) and click **Next**. Select the investment account from the **Account Name** drop-down list and click **Next**.

7 Enter the **Number of Shares**, **Cost Per Share**, and **Commission/Fee** and click **Next**.

8 Verify the security information, and then click **Next**. Leave **No** selected and click **Next**. Click **No** and **Done** to finish setting up investments.

End Task

Task 3: Entering Investment Transactions

Buying, Selling, and Working with Your Investments

You can perform a number of different *actions* with your investment—buy shares, sell shares, receive a dividend, receive more shares as a result of a stock split, and so on. For each action, you enter a corresponding transaction in the investment account register.

✓ **Getting an Action**
The Easy Actions menu on the investment account register toolbar offers more than a dozen different transaction actions.

✓ **Transferring Actions**
When an action name ends with **X** (as in *BuyX*), the action also transfers cash to or from the linked checking account. Before you buy a stock, make sure you enter a deposit transaction for the needed cash into the checking account.

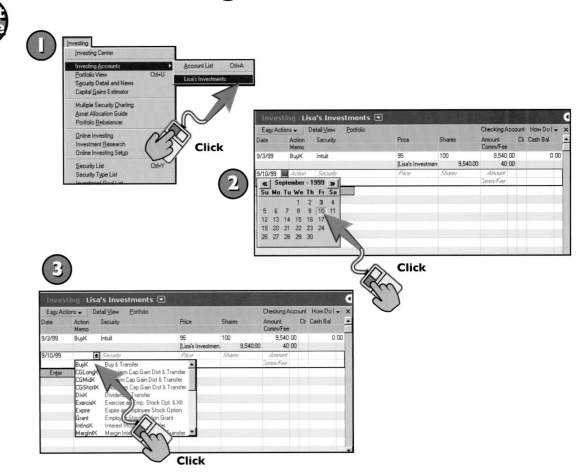

Start Here

Click

Click

Click

1. Choose **Investing**, **Investing Accounts**, then click the name of the investment account to open.

2. Type the action date (mm/dd/yy format) or click the calendar button and click the correct date.

3. Click the **Action** field and then click the desired action.

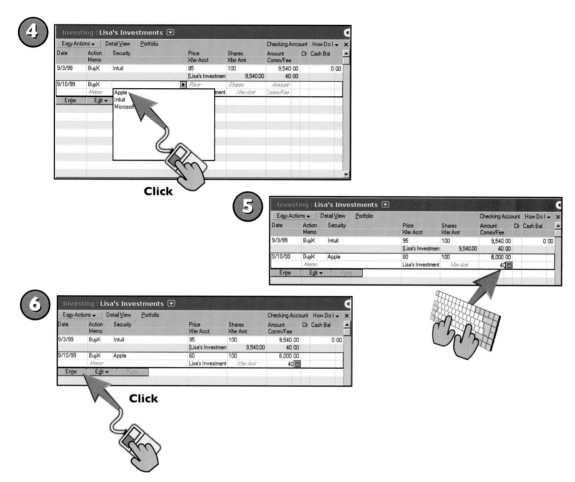

Leaving Transaction Fields Blank

After you make your choice from the **Action field**, Quicken changes the rest of the new transaction line to include only the fields needed for the action you specified. For example, for a dividend action, you only have to specify a Security, Amount, and (optionally) Memo. For a buy or sell transaction, you need to fill in the Price, Shares, Comm/Fee (commission or fee), and Memo fields; Quicken calculates the Xfer Amt (transfer amount) and Amount (total for the transaction) for you.

WARNING
None of the examples shown in this book depict actual security prices.

Other Steps
Quicken might prompt you to provide additional information when you click Enter to finish the transaction.

Click

4️⃣ Click in the **Security** field and then click the desired security.

5️⃣ Enter the transaction information in the needed fields.

6️⃣ Click the **Enter** button below the new transaction line to finish entering the transaction.

Seeing Your Securities

You can display the Portfolio View window when you want to see a list of your securities and update prices to see whether your portfolio has gained or lost in value. You switch to the Portfolio View from the investment account register.

✓ Stock Lots

A *lot* represents the shares of a security that you purchase in a single transaction. If you buy 50 shares of a stock one day, it's the first lot. Buy 100 more the second day, and it becomes another lot.

✓ Reconciling

If your investment account also tracks cash, don't forget to reconcile it. Click **Checking Account** on the Investment Account window toolbar. Then click **Reconcile** on the toolbar to start the process. See Part 3, Tasks 1–5, to learn more about reconciliation.

Task 4: Viewing Securities in the Portfolio View

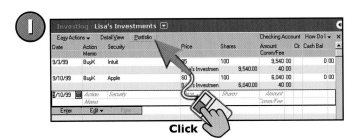

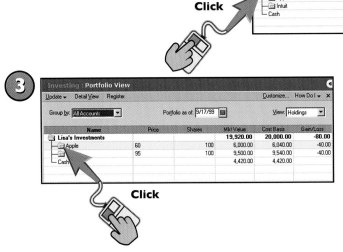

Click

Click

Click

1 Click the **Portfolio** button on the Investment register toolbar.

2 If the list of securities does not appear, click the folder icon beside the account name to open it.

3 To see the lots for a stock, click the folder icon beside the security name.

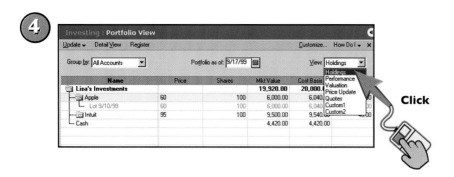

Click

Understanding the Gain/Loss Calculation

The gains and losses Quicken calculates reflect changes in share price, the current number of shares, and commission or fee only. Quicken transfers cash from dividends or security sales back to the linked checking account. You'll learn to update stock prices for gain/loss calculations in the next task.

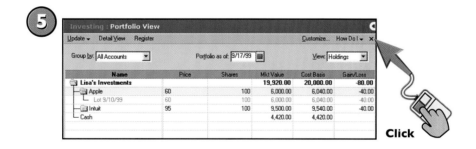

Click

✓ **Real Profits**
To see and print a performance report (earnings from dividends, profits from security sales, and increase in portfolio value), choose **Reports, Investing, Investment Performance Report.**

④ To view other portfolio facts, open the **View** drop-down list and select the information to view.

⑤ Click **Close (X)** button to close the Portfolio View window.

✓ **Back to the Register**
To return to the Investment account register without closing the Portfolio View window, click **Register** on the Portfolio View window toolbar.

End Task

Task 5: Updating a Share Price

Tracking Actual Changing Share Prices

The current share price is one vital piece of information about a security that you can't enter as a transaction; yet the current value of your portfolio hinges totally on accurate share prices. This means you need to update the share price for each security from time to time. If you want to view performance information about your portfolio, as described in Task 4, update the share prices first.

✓ Closing Price
To track your results as your brokerage does, you should enter the closing price for each stock, not an intraday price.

✓ Price Display
After you enter a new price and close the Price History window, the Portfolio View immediately displays the updated share price.

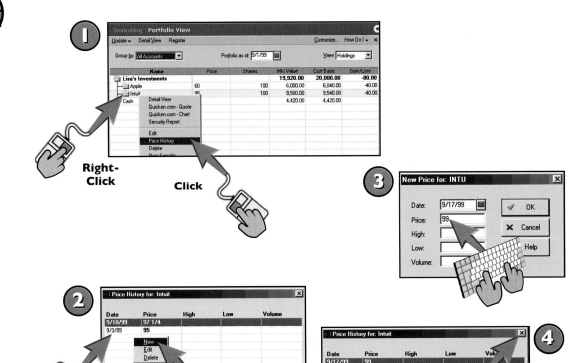

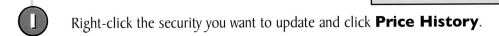

1 Right-click the security you want to update and click **Price History**.

2 Right-click in the Price History For window, and then click **New**.

3 Specify the date and closing price. Optionally, make entries in the text boxes for **High** (price), **Low** (price), and **Volume** (shares traded). Click **OK**.

4 Click the **Close** (**X**) button on the Price History For window.

Next Step

Downloading Quotes from the Internet

Quicken Deluxe 2000's Online Quotes and News feature enables you to retrieve from the Internet the price for nearly any publicly traded security with a ticker symbol not ending in **XX**. Quicken retrieves quotes for all of the securities in your portfolio and typically enters the current price (if the market's open), as well as closing prices for four prior trading days. Start the process in the Portfolio View window.

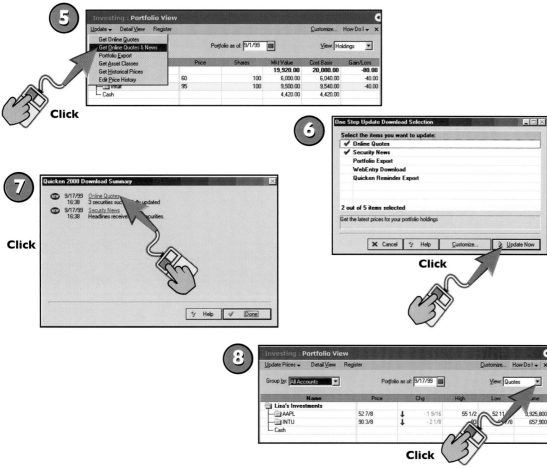

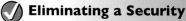

⑤ Click **Update** and click **Get Online Quotes & News**. At the introduction, click **Continue**, specify the desired options, and then click **OK**.

⑥ Click to check or uncheck items to download, if needed, and then click **Update Now**.

⑦ Wait for the data to be downloaded. After the download, click **Online Quotes**.

⑧ After reviewing the quote information, you can use the **View** drop-down list to leave the Quotes information showing, if needed.

✅ **Eliminating a Security**
You can exclude a security from online updating. Choose **Investing, Investing Activities, Set Up My Quotes and News Download**. Click a security to remove the check beside it, and then click **OK**.

Advantages of Managing Investments with Quicken

At first, using an investment account to track your stocks, mutual funds, and other investments might seem a little redundant with the paper statement you receive. Quicken gives you more information than your account statements. You've already seen how you can view account and security performance information. If you want to view performance and history information about a security, you can use the Security Detail View window.

✓ Details, Details

The more share price changes you enter or download, the more detailed your graphs will appear. You choose whether you want to enter share price changes once or twice a month, weekly, or even daily.

Task 6: Using Security Detail View

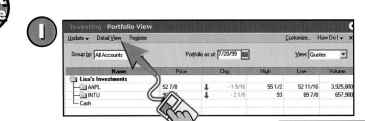

Click

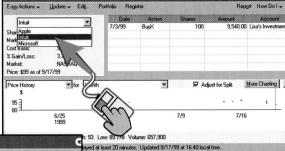

Click

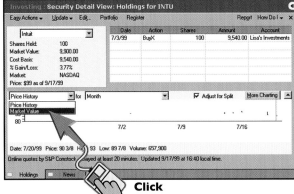

Click

1 Click the **Detail View** button on the Portfolio View window or investment account register toolbar.

2 To view information about a different security, select it from the drop-down list.

3 To graph the value of your holdings over time rather than the security's price history, select **Market Value** from the left midscreen drop-down list.

Next Step

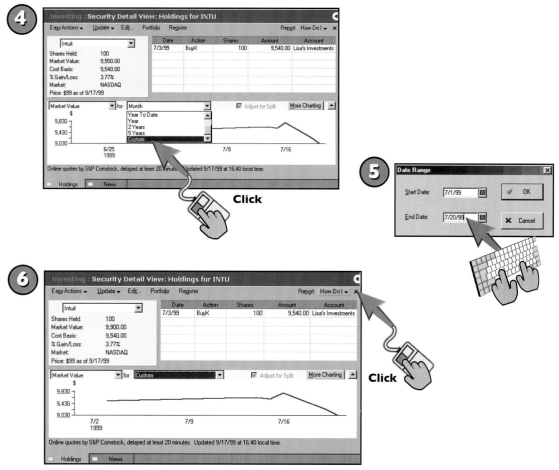

Reading News Downloaded from the Internet

If you used **Online Quotes & News**, you can review downloaded news about the currently displayed security via the Security Detail View window. Click the **News** tab near the bottom of the window. Click the link to the story you want to read. Read the story, click the window **Close (X)** button, and select another story. When you finish, click the **Holdings** tab in the Security Detail View window. To hang up your Internet connection, double-click the connection icon in the system **tray** and click **Disconnect**.

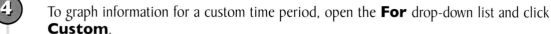

To graph information for a custom time period, open the **For** drop-down list and click **Custom**.

Specify both start and end dates, and click **OK**.

Click the **Close (X)** button to close the Security Detail View window.

 **Backing Up**
To move between the Security Detail View window and another investment window, click either **Portfolio** or **Register** on the Security Detail View window toolbar.

Task 7: Creating a Credit Card Account

Tracking Credit Card Transactions

Although you can track amounts you pay to a credit card company when you pay the credit card bill from your Quicken checking account, this doesn't enable you to categorize each purchase on the bill. To be able to track each separate purchase you make with a particular credit card, you need to create a credit card account for that card in Quicken. To set up the credit card account, you'll need your most recent statement for the account.

✓ Debit Card

If you have a bank debit card that deducts cash directly from your checking account, you enter those transactions in the checking account register. You don't have to create a credit card account for such a card, even though it might carry a Visa or MasterCard logo.

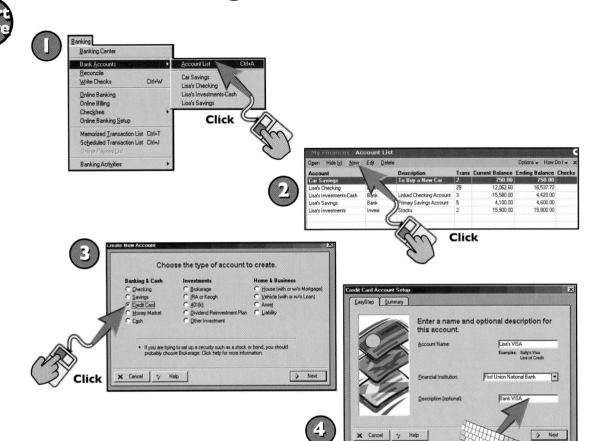

① Choose **Banking**, **Bank Accounts**, **Account List** (**Ctrl+A**) to display the Account List.

② Click the **New** button on the Account List window toolbar.

③ Click the **Credit Card** option button, and then click **Next**.

④ Specify an **Account Name**, **Financial Institution**, and **Description**, and then click **Next**.

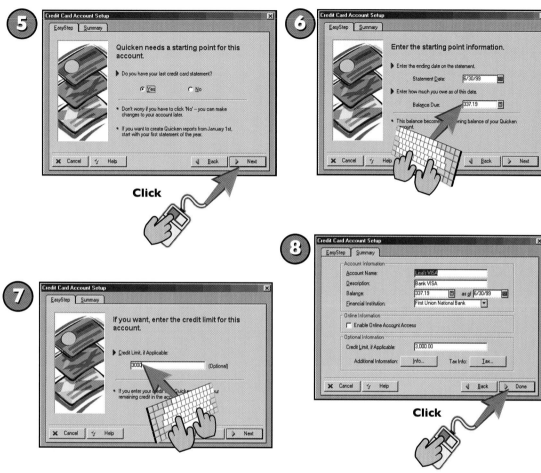

Working with Credit Information Online

If you already know that your credit card company allows online access and you opt to select **Yes** when asked about online access in step 6, see Part 6 to learn more about working online. Although Part 6 focuses on transferring bank account information into Quicken, the overall preparation and download process is the same for a credit card account.

✓ Online Prompt

After you set up your first credit card account, Quicken might ask if you want to learn how to save time when entering transactions. If you click Yes, it can connect you to the Internet so you can check if your credit card company allows you to download account information into Quicken. Click No to skip this process.

---

5 Get your last bank statement for the account, leave **Yes** selected, and click **Next**.

6 Enter the **Statement Date** and **Balance Due**, and click **Next**. Leave **No** selected to decline online access setup, and click **Next** again.

7 Enter any **Credit Limit** that applies to the account, and click **Next**.

8 Verify and correct the account information, and click **Done** to finish opening your new account.

Recording Purchases

Every time you make a purchase with your credit card or get a cash advance, you should enter a transaction documenting the purchase in your credit card account. You enter the purchase transaction in the new transaction line, the first available line in the register. The credit account register uses fields appropriate for credit card transactions. When you finish working with the credit card account, click the **Close (X)** button on the account window to close it.

✓ Special Credit Transactions

If your credit card company sends you checks you can write (instead of charging), enter the check number in the **Ref** field for the transactions. If you're entering a cash advance transaction, select a cash-related category from the **Category** field drop-down list.

Task 8: Entering Credit Card Transactions

Start Here

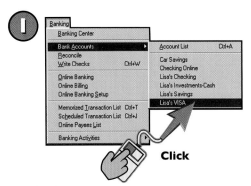

Click

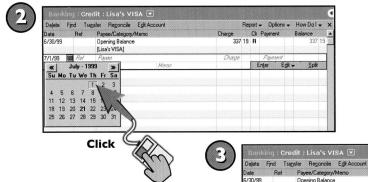

Click

1. Choose **Banking**, **Bank Accounts**, and click the credit card account name.

2. Type the transaction **Date** (mm/dd/yy format) or click the calendar button and click the correct date.

3. Make entries as needed in the **Ref**, **Payee**, and **Charge** (amount of your purchase) fields.

Next Step

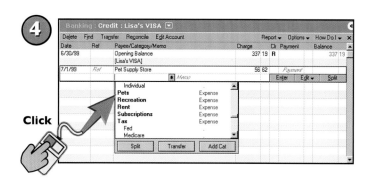

Click

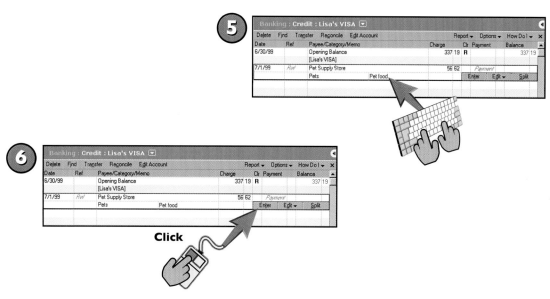

Click

Paying the Bill

Before writing a check to pay your credit card bill, you should reconcile the account. Start the process by clicking the **Reconcile** button on the credit card register window toolbar. Complete the reconciliation, which works much as described in the first five tasks of Part 3. At the end of the process, Quicken prompts you to write a check from a checking account to pay the bill. If you follow the onscreen instructions for doing so, Quicken correctly enters the payment transactions in both the checking account and your credit card account.

✔ Splitting It

You can split any credit card transaction just as you would split a checking account transaction—by clicking the **Split** button below the new transaction line. See Part 1, Task 14, to learn how to split a transaction.

④ Click to open the **Category** field drop-down list, and click the category you want to use.

⑤ Enter a **Memo** field entry, if any.

⑥ Click the **Enter** button below the new transaction line to finish entering the transaction.

End Task

Task 9: Creating a Loan Account

Tracking a Liability

When you borrow money from a person or financial institution, you usually take out a loan—a formal agreement to pay the lender back. That loan debt is a *liability*. In Quicken, setting up a loan simultaneously sets up a liability account to track your payment progress. Quicken leads you through the process of setting up the loan and liability account in Quicken. You'll need to know how much you owe on the loan, how many loan payments you owe, and what the interest rate is. The example here shows how to set up a loan (and corresponding liability account) for a new loan. Quicken leads you through slightly different steps if you choose to enter a loan for which you've already made payments.

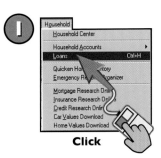

Click

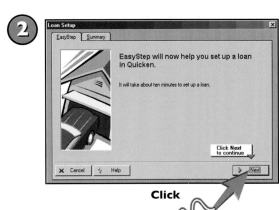

Click

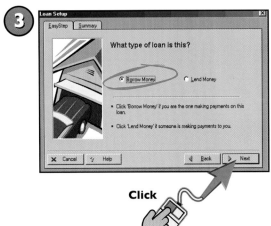

Click

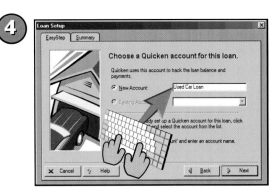

① Choose **Household, Loans (Ctrl+H)**. If this is your first loan, you see a Welcome to Quicken's Loan window; click **Next**. Or, if this is not your first loan, click the **New** button.

② At the EasyStep intro window, click **Next**.

③ Leave **Borrow Money** selected and click **Next**.

④ Enter a liability account name in the **New Account** text box and click **Next**. To continue, click **No** and then **Next**.

Next Step

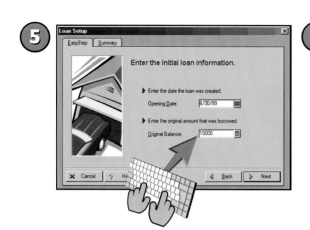

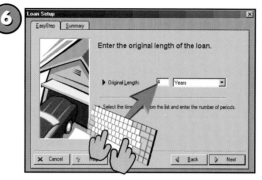

Click

Telling Quicken How Much You Owe

Most lenders refer to the amount left to pay on a loan as the *principal balance*. If you're entering a new loan, you'll know what this amount is; however, for a loan on which you've already made payments, you'll need to look around. The principal balance figure usually appears on your home mortgage bill, but might not appear on a payment slip for a personal or car loan. In such a case, call the lending institution to find out the correct account balance.

5 Enter the loan's **Opening Date** and **Original Balance** and click **Next**. Leave **No** selected and click **Next** again.

6 Enter the loan's **Original Length** and click **Next**. Accept the **Standard Period** and **Compounding Period** by clicking **Next** twice.

7 Specify the **Date of First Payment** and click **Next**. Click **No** and **Next** to have Quicken calculate the first payment.

8 Enter an **Interest Rate** and click **Next**. Click **Next** twice and **Done** to verify the summary information. Then continue to the next task in this book.

 **First Payment**
The loan setup process includes setting up the loan payments. Move on to Task 10 to see how to continue the process beyond the steps here.

Task 10: Setting Up and Making Loan Payments

Finishing the Payment Setup

If you followed the procedure described in the last task to set up your loan and its liability account, you told Quicken to calculate upcoming payments for you. The amount Quicken calculates should match the amount calculated by your financial institution, but Quicken gives you the chance to verify that and change the payment amount, if needed.

✓ Adding an Asset Account

After you finish setting up the payment, Quicken asks if you want to set up an asset account to track how much value you're building as you pay off the loan. You can click **Yes** if you want to do so, but you typically only need to do so when the loan is for something that grows in value (such as a home), rather than something that loses value (such as a car).

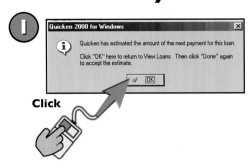

Click

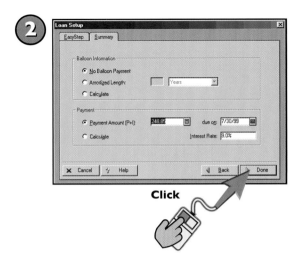

Click

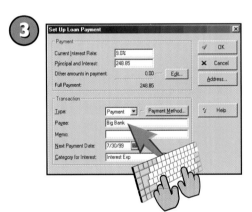

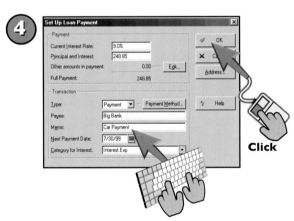

Click

In the message box, click **OK** to proceed with setting up the loan payment.

Click **Done** to close the final summary screen from the loan setup.

Edit any of the information Quicken calculated and then enter the **Payee** (lender).

Enter a **Memo** and then click **OK**. When the Asset Account Setup dialog box appears, click **No**.

Next Step

Click

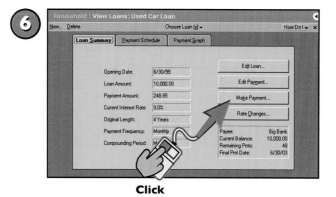

Click

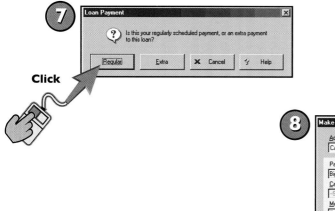

Click

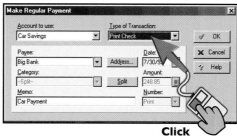

Click

Making a Loan Payment

After you set up the loan and the loan account, you use the View Loans window to enter each loan payment. Specify the checking account to use to pay the payment. Quicken automatically enters the check transaction in that checking account. It also enters a corresponding transaction in the liability account. This second transaction decreases the liability balance by the principal amount from the payment.

---

⑤ If the View Loans window doesn't appear, choose **Household**, **Loans (Ctrl+H)**. Use the **Choose Loan** button to display another loan, if needed.

⑥ Click **Make Payment**.

⑦ Click **Regular** to verify that you're making a regular payment.

⑧ Select the **Account to Use** and the **Type of Transaction**, update any other payment information, and click **OK**.

Choose a Loan
If you've created multiple loans in Quicken, you need to choose the loan to pay in the View Loans window. To do so, click the **Choose Loan** button on the window toolbar and click the loan to use.

Task 11: Tracking a 401(k)

Setting Up a 401(k) Account

You store most investments—even IRA contributions—in a regular investment account; however, a 401(k) requires some special tracking features. As a result, you need to set up a 401(k) plan a little differently. Before you start, grab the last 401(k) statement you received. You'll need information from it to correctly set up the Quicken 401(k) account.

✅ 401 What?
A 401(k) is an employer-sponsored investment plan to which you can make contributions before taxes and into which your employer can make matching contributions.

❗ WARNING
The number of securities you enter are the number of different stocks or mutual funds in the account, not the number of shares in each investment.

Start Here

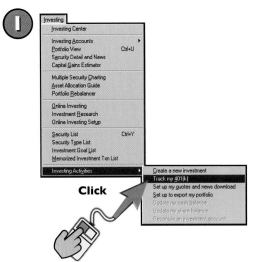

Click

Click

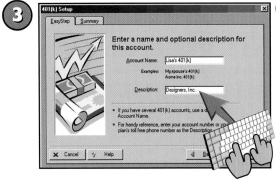

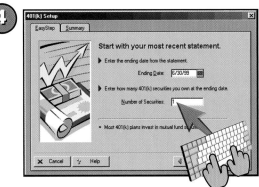

1 Choose **Investing**, **Investing Activities**, **Track My 401(k)**.

2 Click **Next** in the Welcome dialog box.

3 Enter an **Account Name** and **Description** and click **Next**.

4 Specify the last statement **Ending Date** and the **Number of Securities** in your account at that time, and click **Next**.

Next Step

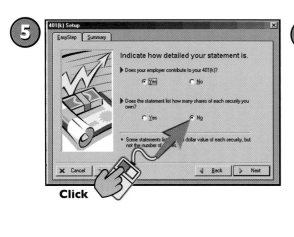

Click

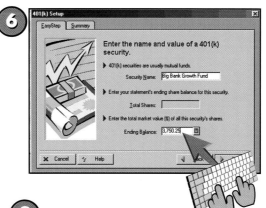

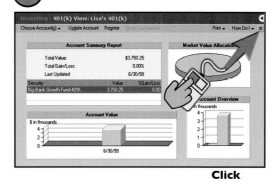

Click

Click

Identifying the Securities

Based on what you entered in the **Number of Securities** text box in step 3, Quicken prompts you to repeat step 5 as many times as needed to set up each security. Depending on your answer to the bottom question in step 4, you might or might not have to make a Total Shares entry in step 5. Many 401(k) plans only list the value of the shares you hold, not the share price.

(5) Click your answers to the next questions asked by 401(k) Setup and then click **Next**.

(6) Enter the **Security Name**, **Ending Balance**, and **Total Shares** (if its text box isn't grayed). Click **Next**.

(7) Verify the account information and click **Done**.

(8) If you've finished reviewing the 401(k) information, click the window **Close** (**X**) button.

Another 401(k)?
To add another 401(k) account, choose **Investing, Investing Accounts, Account List (Ctrl+A)**. Click the **New** button on the toolbar, click the 401(k) choice, click **Next**, and finish the account setup process.

End Task

Task 12: Updating a 401(k)

Entering Statement Information

Each time you receive a 401(k) statement, which usually occurs quarterly, you need to update your 401(k) account in Quicken to reflect the recent additions, as described here.

Start Here

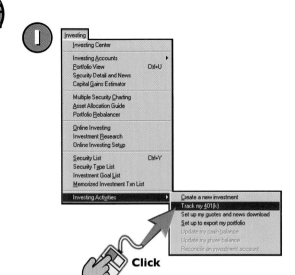

Click

Click

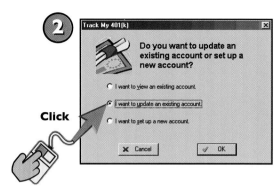

Click

✓ Checking Out the 401(k)

You have to open the 401(k) View window to see what's in your 401(k) and how much you've gained. To view your 401(k) information later, choose **Investing, Investing Accounts,** and then click the name of the 401(k) account. Click the **401(k) View** button to view the account information graphically. Choose the account to view from the **Choose Account** drop-down list. Click the **Close (X)** button for the 401(k) View window to close it.

Click

① Choose **Investing, Investing Activities, Track My 401(k)**.

② Click **I Want to Update an Existing Account**, and then click **OK**.

③ If you've created more than one 401(k) account, select the correct one from the **Account Name** drop-down list and click **OK**.

④ Enter the statement ending date in the **This Statement Ends** text box and click **Next**.

Next Step

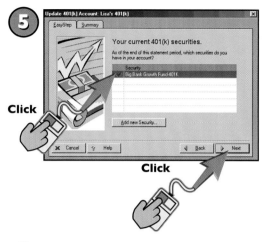

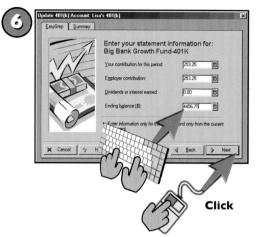

Automating 401(k) Deposits

You can run Paycheck Setup (see Part 2, Task 14) and set up your scheduled paycheck transaction to enter your 401(k) deposit automatically. Create your 401(k) account before you set up your paycheck to deposit to it.

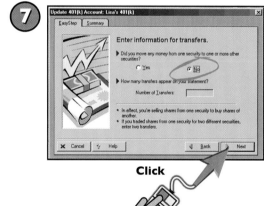

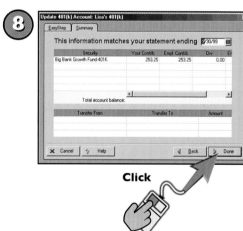

✅ **Another Security**
You can click the **Add New Security** button (see step 5) to enter information about another security you're investing in within your 401(k) account.

✅ **Securities Transfers**
If you reallocated some of your investment from one security to another, click Yes in step 7 and enter the **Number of Transfers**. Then, when prompted, enter the **Transfer Amount, From Security,** and **To Security** information for each transfer.

⑤ If needed, click to remove the check mark beside any security you no longer hold, and then click **Next**.

⑥ Enter the appropriate statement information and click **Next**. (Repeat this step for each security, when prompted.)

⑦ Leave **No** selected and click **Next**.

⑧ Verify the update information and then click **Done**.

Adding Stock Options to an Investment Account

New features in Quicken Deluxe 2000 streamline the process for tracking employee stock options (the ability to purchase company stock at a particular price that's typically below the market price). You track stock options in an investment account. You should use the process described in Task 1 of this part to set up an investment account to hold option information before completing this task. As described in Task 2, Quicken prompts you to add a security to the new account. At that point, go to step 3 of this task.

✓ A New Stock

You create a new security while adding the option. To do so, click the **A New Stock** option button in step 4, then enter the stock **Name** and **Ticker Symbol**.

Task 13: Tracking Stock Options

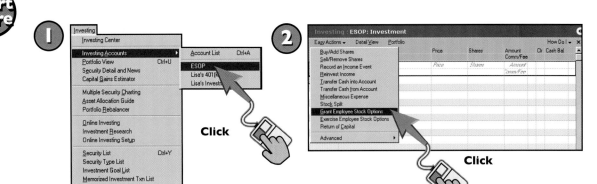

Click

Click

Click

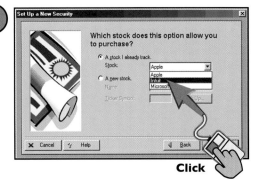

Click

① Choose **Investing**, **Investing Accounts**, and then click the name of the account to hold the options to open it.

② Choose **Grant Employee Stock Options** from the **Easy Actions** menu on the register window toolbar.

③ In the Set Up a New Security dialog box, click the **Employee Stock Option** option button, and then click **Next**.

④ To create an option for a security you've already entered in Quicken, choose it from the **Stock** drop-down list and click **Next**.

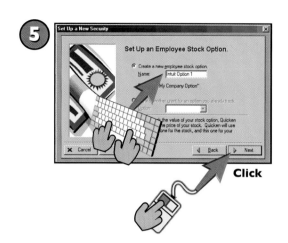

Click

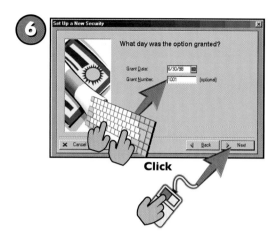

Click

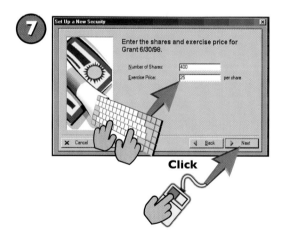

Click

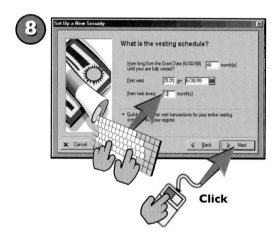

Click

Finishing the Option Grant

You'll need to know how many options you have and how those options vest, or become active so you can enter the option grant properly. You also need to know the option price, the special price at which you can use (exercise) the option and make your stock purchase. After you finish entering the option, the investment account register includes a transaction for each option vesting date.

Still More Options
If you're adding an additional option grant for an option you've previously entered, click the **Create Another Grant for an Option You Already Track** choice in step 5, then choose the appropriate option from the **Option** drop-down list.

(5) Edit the option name in the **Name** text box and then click **Next**.

(6) Enter the **Grant Date** and **Grant Number** and then click **Next**.

(7) Enter the **Number of Shares** and **Exercise Price** and then click **Next**.

(8) Enter the vesting information and then click **Next**. Enter expiration information, click **Next** twice, and then click **No**, **Next**, **No**, and **Done**, respectively, to finish.

End Task

Task 14: Updating Stock Options

Exercising the Stock Option

After stock option shares vest, you can exercise your option to purchase those shares. When you do so, you need to enter information into the applicable investment account to reflect the purchase of those shares. Once again, the latest version of Quicken automates this process to make it speedy.

⊘ Is It Qualified?

When you have a qualified option, you don't have to pay income tax until you *sell* the shares you purchased via the option. If you have a non-qualified option, you pay tax when you exercise the option, or *buy* shares via the option. Make sure you know what type of options you have to enter option information correctly and to ensure proper tax treatment.

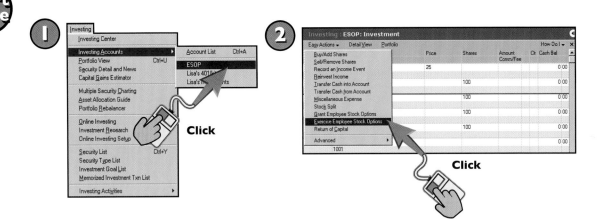

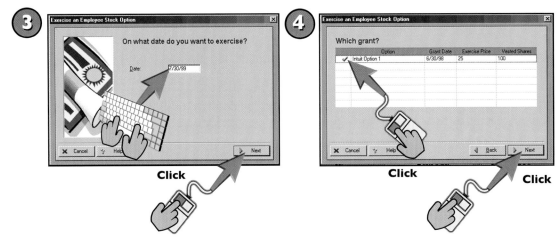

1. Choose **Investing**, **Investing Accounts**, and click the name of the account to hold the options to open it.

2. Choose **Exercise Employee Stock Options** from the **Easy Actions** menu on the register window toolbar.

3. Enter the exercise (purchase) **Date** and then click **Next**.

4. If needed, click the option name to check it, and then click **Next**.

Next
Step

5

Click

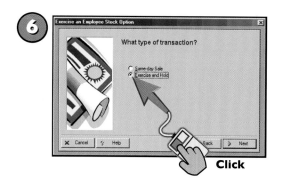

6

Click

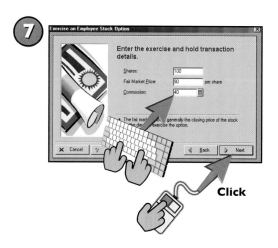

7

Click

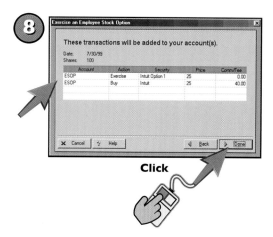

8

Click

Updating the Stock Values

As you enter the information about how you exercised the option, you need to specify whether you will exercise the option and hold the stock you purchase, or use a same-day sale to take your profits immediately. If you incur any broker commissions for the transaction(s), be sure you have accurate commission information on hand to continue.

✓ Updating the Stock Values
Quicken adds stock options you enter to your securities list. When you update securities online as described in Task 5 of this part, it updates the option values, too. You also can view your options in the Security Detail View, described earlier.

5 Click the option button for the appropriate option type and then click **Next**.

6 Click the option button for the appropriate transaction type and then click **Next**.

7 Enter the information about the transaction (the entries vary depending on your choice in Step 6), and then click **Next**.

8 If needed, select the account which will hold the shares, and click **Next**. Review the transaction information, and click **Done**.

End Task

Using Quicken as a Planning Tool

So far you've used Quicken to capture information and look at your financial history. This part shows you how to use Quicken to look at your financial future—how to budget, plan for tax time, and calculate how much to save to meet a need down the road.

Tasks

Task 1: Setting Up Your First Budget

Determining How Much You Want to Save

Your *budget* captures income and expenses you expect to have. If you plan your budget accurately, you'll be able to anticipate discretionary dollars available for other purposes. You might save for a particular purchase on a particular date, for example. In addition, an accurate budget can help you pin down specific categories where you'd like to reduce spending, such as economizing on groceries.

✅ **Automatic Budgeting**
If you've already entered several months' worth of transactions in Quicken, click the **Edit** button on the Budget window tool bar and then click **Autocreate**.

✅ **Choosing Categories**
Include all of the categories used in your scheduled and memorized transactions in the budget, as well as any other categories you use frequently for transactions.

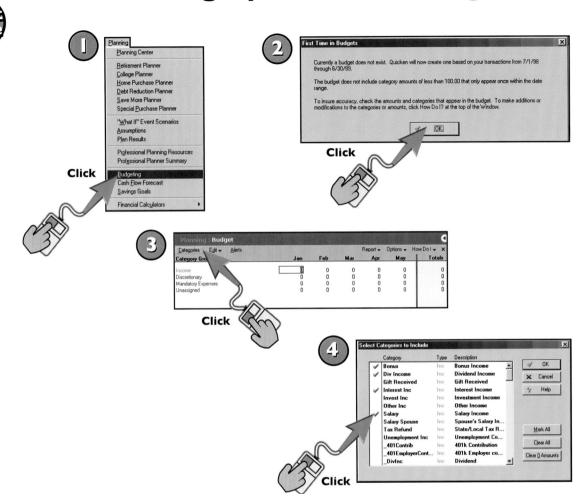

Start Here

Click

Click

Click

Click

1. Choose **Planning**, **Budgeting**.

2. If the First Time in Budgets dialog box appears, click **OK**.

3. Click the **Categories** button on the Budget window toolbar.

4. Click to check each category to include in the budget, and then click **OK**.

Next Step

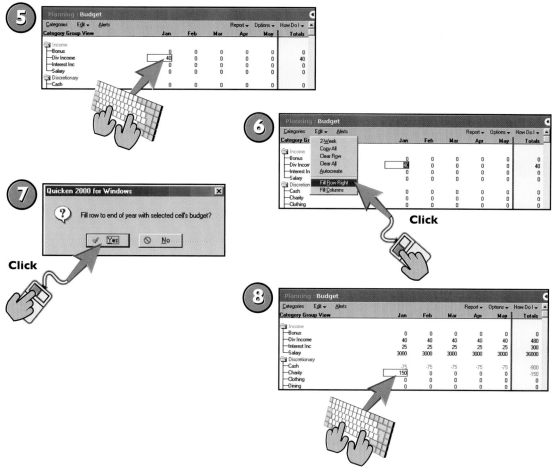

Click

Click

Filling Budget Amounts

Your budget should be as on target as possible, but it's not necessary to estimate every monthly expense to the penny. The best approach is to enter a round number for each category in the first month of the budget and "fill" that number to subsequent months. You can go back and adjust values for one-time events, such as a month when you expect to receive a bonus or a month when you expect a car insurance payment. As you build your budget, watch the budget figures calculated at the bottom of the Budget window.

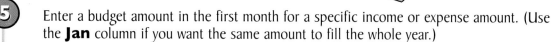

(5) Enter a budget amount in the first month for a specific income or expense amount. (Use the **Jan** column if you want the same amount to fill the whole year.)

(6) Click the **Edit** button on the Budget window toolbar, and then click **Fill Row Right**.

(7) Click **Yes** to finish the fill.

(8) To edit an individual amount, click the amount, type the new amount, and then press **Enter**.

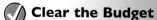

✅ **Clear the Budget**
To clear a single row, click the row you want. Then click **Edit** on the Budget window toolbar and click **Clear Row**. To clear the whole budget, click **Edit** and then click **Clear All**.

End Task

Task 2: Saving and Displaying Budgets

Saving the Current and New Budgets

Any time you enter information in or make changes to a budget, you need to save the budget. Saving is a one-step operation that doesn't take long, unlike entering dozens of figures into a budget. To keep a budget easier to work with by tracking fewer categories or to create a budget for each new year, you can create multiple budget files. In addition to covering how to save a budget, this task also shows you how to create a new budget file.

✓ How Many Budgets?

You could create a budget to show only certain categories, such as a budget for car expenses. You could create a budget to track how much your child is spending at college, or create a new budget for each year.

Start Here

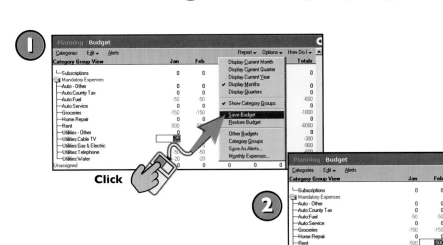

Click

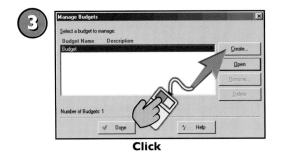

Click

Click

① Click the **Options** button on the Budget window toolbar, and then click **Save Budget**.

② Click the **Options** button on the Budget window toolbar, and then click **Other Budgets**.

③ In the Manage Budgets window, click **Create**.

④ In the Create Budget window, enter the budget name and description, make a choice under **Create Budget Options**, and then click **OK**.

Next Step

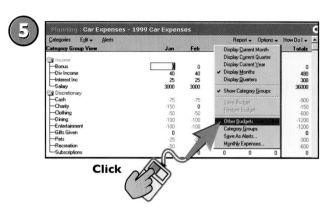

Click

Displaying Another Budget

With the Budget window displayed, you can display any previously created budget. To display a report or graph of a budget's information, you have to open that budget in the Budget window. Remember to save your budget before displaying another budget.

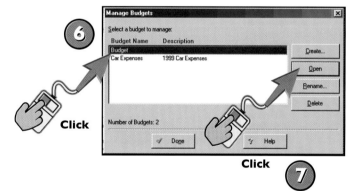

Click

Click

5 Click the **Options** button on the Budget window toolbar, and then click **Other Budgets**.

6 Click the budget you want to open.

7 Click **Open**.

✓ **Other Categories**
To adjust the categories in a new budget, use the **Categories** button on the Budget window toolbar.

✓ **Back to Budgets**
If the Budget window isn't open, choose **Planning, Budgeting** to redisplay it.

Displaying a Budget Report

After you set up your budgets, you can later open the budget in the Budget window and generate and print a report. The report shows you how actual income and expenses (totaled from transactions you entered) compare with the budget amounts you entered. You can choose either the Budget Report, which shows the year-to-date budgeted and actual figures, or the Monthly Budget Report, which compares monthly budgeted versus actual amounts for each category. After you display a report, you can print it, too.

✓ **Report Adjustments**
You can modify a Budget report just like any other. See Part 3, Task 8, to learn how to modify a report.

Task 3: Comparing Budgeted Versus Actual Expenses

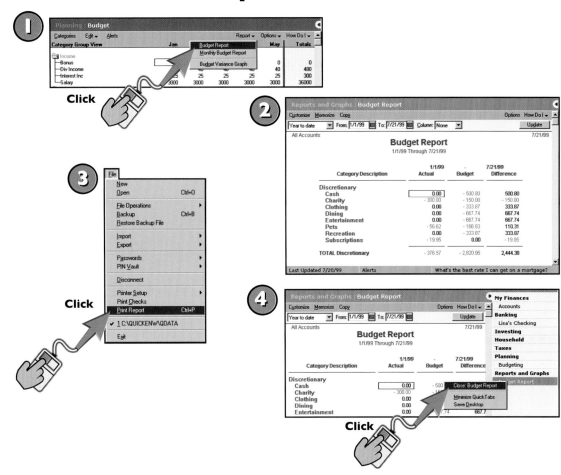

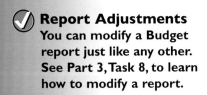

(1) Open the **Report** menu on the Budget window toolbar. Then click the name of the report you want to display.

(2) Review the **Actual**, **Budget**, and **Difference** columns to see how you're doing.

(3) To print the budget, choose **File**, **Print Report** (**Ctrl+P**) and click **OK**.

(4) Display the QuickTab column, right-click the report name, then click **Close: Report Name** to close the Budget report window. Hide the QuickTab column.

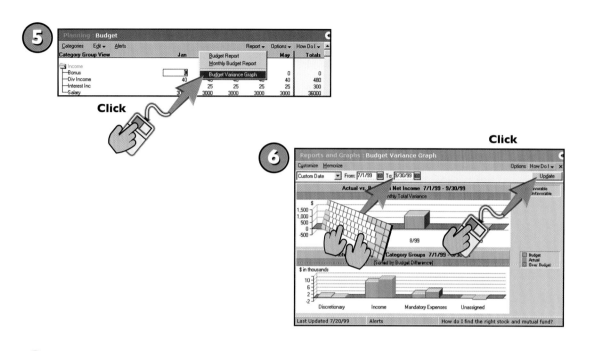

Click

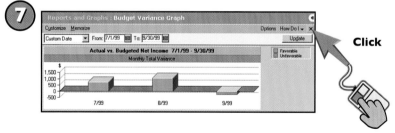

Click

Graphing Your Budgeting Results

Rather than displaying a budget report, you can display an attractive graph of your budgeted versus actual results. The graph illustrates the budget comparison for the year to date, so you can see at a glance where you've exceeded or stayed within your budget. Before you use the steps on this page, display the budget to graph in the **Budget window.**

Click

5 Open the **Report** menu on the Budget window toolbar, and then click **Budget Variance Graph**.

6 To graph a different time period, enter new **From** and **To** dates, and then click the **Update** button.

7 Click the **Close (X)** button to close the Budget Variance Graph window.

✓ **Family Affair**
Share budget results, especially the easy-to-understand graph, with everyone in the household. You might convince skeptics to join you in your quest for better budget management.

✓ **Graph Changes**
See Part 3, Task 9, to learn how to adjust a Quicken graph.

End Task

Task 4: Setting Up for Tax Planning

Specifying Tax Categories

For Quicken to track Federal tax information accurately, you need to tell it which transaction categories identify tax information. After you identify *tax-related categories*, Quicken can display a report that totals all transactions using these categories. Use these calculated figures to reduce your tax preparation time. Quicken by default identifies many categories as tax-related (such as the **Salary** and **Charity** categories), but you should double-check to ensure all tax-related categories are marked as such, especially if you've created any categories or subcategories.

✓ **Tax Report**
To display the report of all tax-related income and expense transactions, choose **Reports, Taxes, Tax Summary Report**.

Start Here

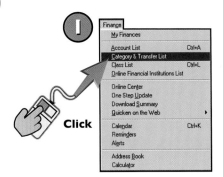

Click

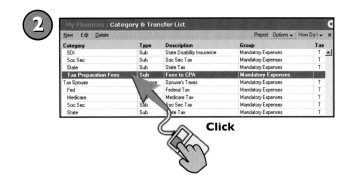

Click

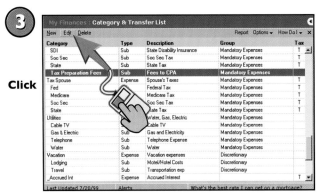

Click

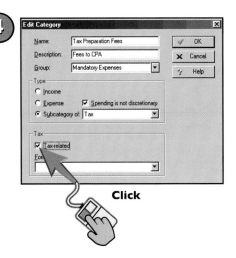

Click

① Choose **Finance**, **Category & Transfer List**.

② Click the category you want to mark as tax-related.

③ Click the **Edit** button on the **Category & Transfer List** window toolbar.

④ Check **Tax-related**.

Next Step

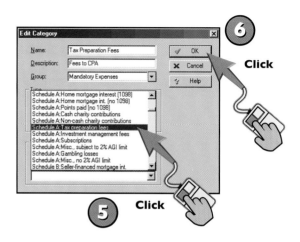

Click

Click

Click

Assigning a Tax Form

If you plan to use Quicken to display an estimate of your Federal taxes for the year, you need to tell Quicken to apply each tax-related category to the correct tax form and line. I suggest dragging out your tax forms and tax booklets from the prior year to help you match the categories and lines. When you receive the tax forms for the current year, you can double-check your categories and repeat steps 1–3 to get started in changing any category.

⑤ In the Edit Category window, open the **Form** drop-down list and click the tax form and line to which the category applies.

⑥ Click **OK**.

⑦ Click the **Close (X)** button to close the Category & Transfer List window.

✓ Estimate It
After you've correctly matched tax-related categories and lines, you can move on to Task 5 to learn how to generate the tax estimate.

Task 5: Displaying a Tax Estimate

Starting the Tax Planner

Quicken's *Tax Planner* can generate an estimate of the taxes you owe for the current year. Even if thinking about taxes in June is painful, doing so can save you money. If you underpay your Federal taxes, you can incur an underpayment penalty. On the flip side, a substantial overpayment leaves you with less money in the bank—and less interest earned—during the year.

 Start Here

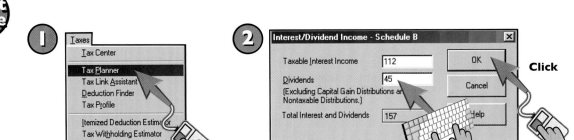

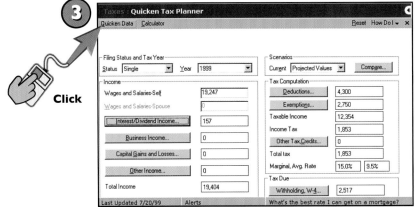

✓ **Need More Deductions?**
See Part 7, Task 4, to learn how Quicken can help you find more tax deductions.

① Choose **Taxes**, **Tax Planner**. If a Tax Law Update window appears, click **OK** to move past it. If a Quicken Help window opens, close it (**X**) or move it if it gets in your way.

② To manually enter a value, type it into a text box. You can also click a button, enter the value(s), and click **OK**.

③ It you want to import your Quicken data, click the **Quicken Data** button on the Tax Planner window toolbar.

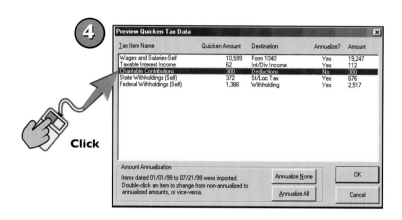

Click

Importing Your Quicken Data into the Tax Planner

As noted in step 2, you can enter values for the Tax Planner to use to generate its estimate. Go this route if it's early in the year and you just want a rough estimate of the taxes you'll owe. However, if you've accumulated quite a bit of Quicken data and have set up the categories to link with tax form lines as explained in Task 4, you can click the Quicken Data button (step 3) to import actual information and base your estimate on real information.

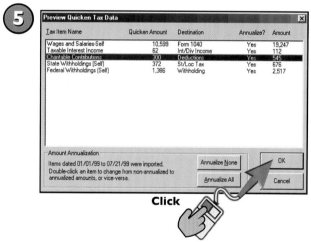

Click

④ If the Annualize column for a category says **No**, double-click that item to change it to **Yes**, or click **Annualize All**.

⑤ Click **OK** to finish and display the tax estimate.

✔ **Annualize Me**
When Tax Planner annualizes a category, it projects a full-year total for that entry based on the sum of the amounts for transactions entered to date.

Playing What-If

After you finish Task 5, the Tax Planner displays a nice, concise summary of your tax information. In its lower right corner, the Planner shows you either a **Tax Due** or **Refund Due** amount; however, the Tax Planner's calculations aren't set in stone. You can adjust different settings and entries to check how much tax you'd owe under different conditions, such as comparing the tax owed when you select the **Married-Joint** (married filing jointly) versus **Married-Sep** (married filing separately) filing status.

✓ **For Further Comparison**
To compare multiple tax scenarios, choose another choice from the **Current** drop-down list near the top of the Tax Planner window. Copy your original entries when prompted, and adjust the settings and entries. Click **Compare.** You can't print the comparison, though.

Task 6: Tweaking and Printing the Tax Estimate

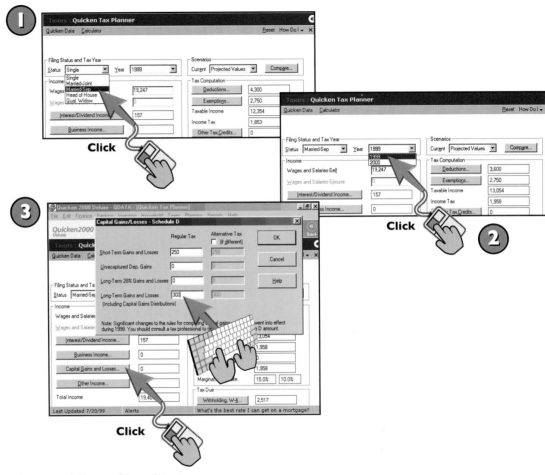

Start Here

Click

Click

Click

1️⃣ Choose a different filing **Status**.

2️⃣ Choose the proper tax **Year**.

3️⃣ To override a value or enter a missing one, type it. You can also click a button, edit the value(s), and click **OK**.

Next Step

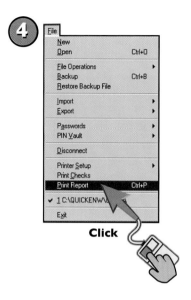

Click

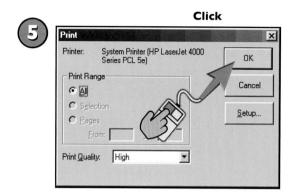

Click

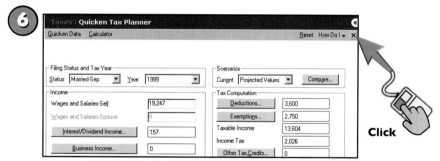

Click

(4) Choose **File**, **Print Report** (**Ctrl+P**).

(5) Click **OK** to send the tax estimate to the printer.

(6) Click the window **Close** (**X**) button to exit Tax Planner.

Printing and Exiting

Although you can redisplay or re-create the Tax Planner calculation, you might want to make a printout. For example, you might want to share the information with a tax planning professional or other financial advisor. After you've printed, you can wrap up your work and close the Tax Planner.

✓ **Withholding Adjustments**
If either the Refund Due or Tax Amount Due calculated by the Tax Planner seems extremely large, contact your employer's Human Resources department and adjust your withholding amounts in the appropriate direction.

✓ **Tax Planning Later**
When you exit the Tax Planner and later restart it, the Planner displays any tax-planning information you previously entered (unless you clicked Reset, that is).

Task 7: Finding More Tax Deductions

Using the Deduction Finder

If you used Task 6 to prepare a tax estimate, you may discover that you'll owe a tax payment at the end of the current tax year. Or, your refund may not be as large as you had expected. You can use Quicken's Deduction Finder to look for potential tax deductions; you may find that you should've been itemizing your deductions all along! The Deduction Finder asks you a series of questions. You respond to the questions to find deductions for which you may be eligible—called your action plan.

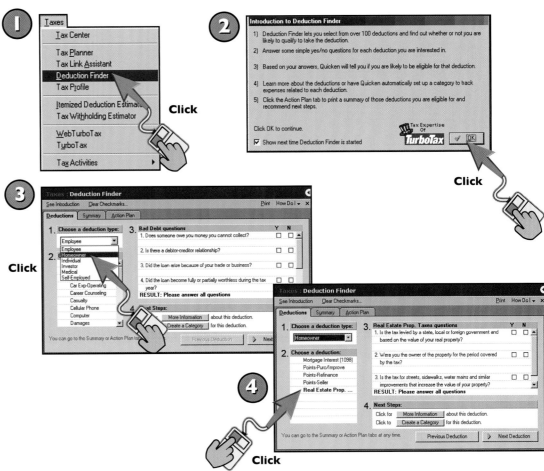

1 Choose **Taxes**, **Deduction Finder**.

2 If you see the Introduction to Deduction Finder dialog box, click **OK**.

3 Make a choice from the **1. Choose a Deduction Type** drop-down list.

4 Click a choice under **2. Choose a Deduction**.

Next Step

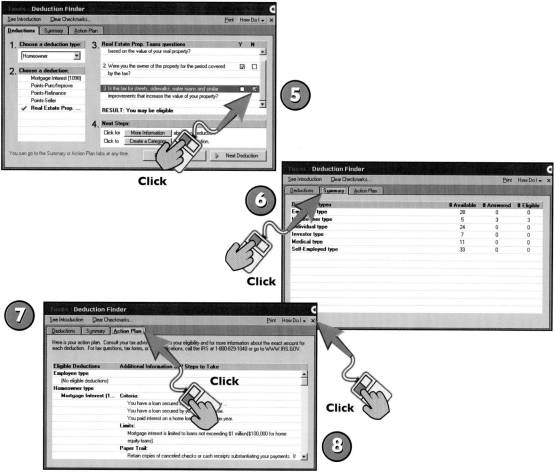

Reviewing Your Action Plan

The Action Plan tab in the Deduction Finder window lists potential deductions for you. Review each of these deductions, and use the File, Print List (Ctrl+P) command to print the action plan for tax time. You can then contact a tax advisor or the IRS (www.irs.gov) to verify whether you can take particular deductions and reduce your tax burden.

Click the **Y** or **N** check box to respond to each of the questions listed for **3. Real Estate Prop. Taxes Questions**.

Repeat steps 3–5 to research additional deductions, then click the **Summary** tab to review a tally of available deductions.

Click the **Action Plan** tab to review your action plan.

Click the window **Close (X)** button to exit Deduction Finder.

Task 8: Using a Financial Calculator

Looking at the Calculators

Quicken offers five different *financial calculators* that can help you anticipate and quantify certain financial needs. The Loan Calculator can figure the monthly payments for a loan at a certain rate. Use the Refinance Calculator to compare different loan refinancing opportunities. Use the Investment Savings Calculator to learn how much you need to deposit or contribute over time to meet a target amount or how much you'll have later at your current rate of savings. Use the College Calculator or Retirement Calculator to determine how much to save now to fund tuition or a life on the beach.

✓ Similarities

Though there are slight differences among the financial calculators, you follow the same process to use each one.

Start Here

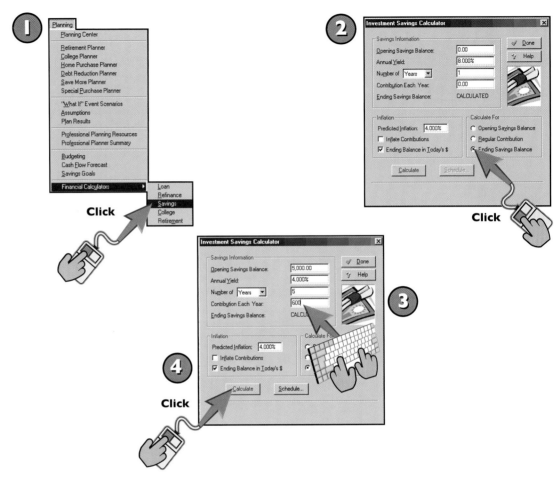

Click

Click

Click

1 Choose **Planning**, **Financial Calculators**, and then click the calculator you want to use.

2 If the Calculator dialog box offers a Calculate For area, click your choice there.

3 Enter or change other values as needed.

4 Click **Calculate** if the Calculator doesn't automatically recalculate the needed amount.

Next Step

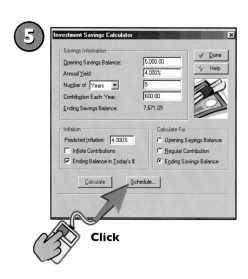

Click

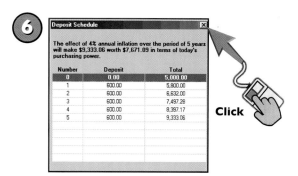

Click

Viewing a Contribution Schedule

You can display a schedule of deposits you need to make (into the account of your choice) to reach a calculated total. You can even print multiple schedules to compare different schedules and totals. When you finish working, you can close the Savings calculator.

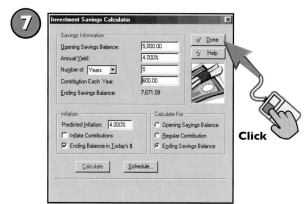

Click

(5) Click the **Schedule** button. (You can do this for all calculators except Refinance; it doesn't have a Schedule button.)

(6) Click the window **Close (X)** button to return to the financial calculator.

(7) Click **Done** to finish working with the financial calculator.

✔ **Life Event Planners**
The Planning menu also offers several life event planners that also help you project needed savings amounts or project savings accumulation. These planners are very interactive, and in some cases are more detailed than the financial planners.

PART 6

Using Quicken Online

The Internet now not only enables you to find financial information online, but it also enables you to handle your banking online. If your bank or brokerage offers the capability, you can download account information directly into Quicken via the Internet, saving you the trouble of entering and updating transactions. You can even pay bills online. This part shows you how to set up for and get started using Quicken's online banking features.

Tasks

Task 1: Entering a Financial Institution

Preparing for Online Access

To use Quicken's online banking features, you need to call your bank and enroll in the service. The bank gives you a Personal Identification Number (PIN) for online access and sends you an enrollment kit. After you receive it, you need to give Quicken information about your financial institution and online access PIN. Tasks 1 and 2 illustrate entering a financial institution and enabling an account for online banking.

✓ On the Net

Online banking features require that you connect to the Internet. To get or set up an Internet account, click the **Start** button and choose **Programs, Internet Explorer, Connection Wizard.** In Quicken, use the **Edit, Internet Connection Setup** command to set up Quicken to work with your Internet connection.

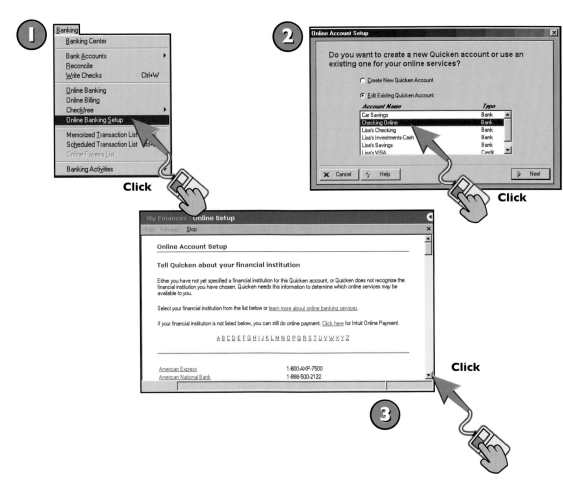

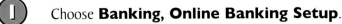

Choose **Banking, Online Banking Setup**.

In the Online Account Setup window, click the name of the account to use for online banking, and then click **Next**.

Scroll down the Online Account Setup list, and click the name of your bank.

Next
Step ▶

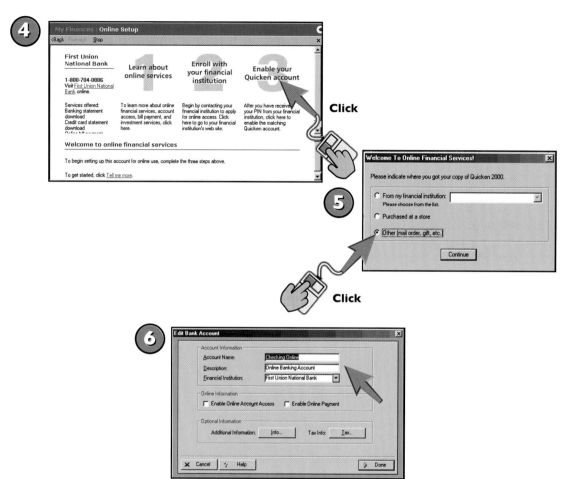

Setting Up an Investing Account for Online Investing

A number of brokerage companies now enable you to download account information into Quicken Deluxe 2000. To set up an investment account you've created for online banking, start the process using the **Investing, Online Investing Setup** command. Pick up with step 2 of this task, selecting the proper brokerage from the list of brokerage companies that appears, and follow to the next setup task, responding to the prompts Quicken displays as needed.

✓ **Free Online Banking**
Typically, banks charge a small monthly fee for online banking; some banks offer the service for free if you have a particular kind of account or maintain a certain balance. Be sure to ask about account changes that could reduce or eliminate your online banking fee.

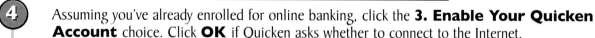

(4) Assuming you've already enrolled for online banking, click the **3. Enable Your Quicken Account** choice. Click **OK** if Quicken asks whether to connect to the Internet.

(5) If prompted, specify where you received Quicken, and then click **Continue**.

(6) After Intuit finishes downloading, it shows you it's ready to set up an account for online banking. Go to the next task.

Task 2: Enabling Online Access for an Account

Continuing Online Financial Services Setup

After you tell Quicken which financial institution you use for online banking, you need to enable the selected account for online banking and provide some account information. This task picks up exactly where Task 1 left off, showing you how to set up the account to receive the information you download into Quicken from your bank or other institution. The steps will differ slightly if you're setting up for credit card or investment tracking. Just supply the information that Quicken asks for in each case.

Click

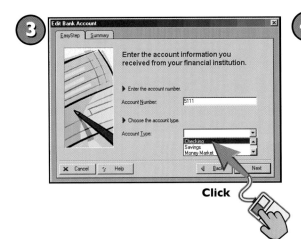

Click

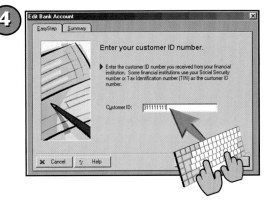

1 Click to check the **Enable Online Account Access** and **Enable Online Payment** check boxes, and then click **Next**.

2 Enter your bank's **Routing Number** (see your enrollment information) and then click **Next**.

3 Enter the **Account Number** and select an **Account Type**. Click **Next**.

4 Enter the **Customer ID** and click **Next**.

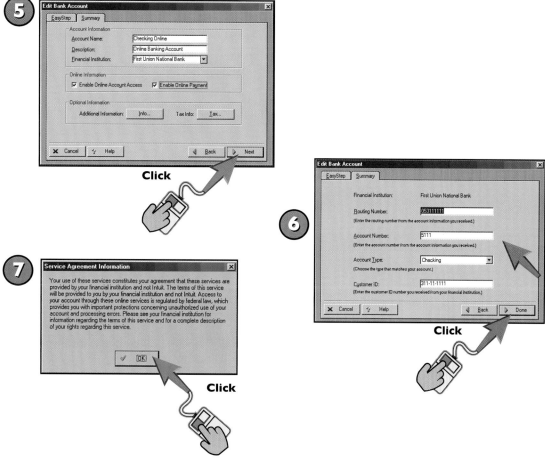

Online Access Account Numbers

The account number you enter for online banking or online investing might differ from the full account number you use for paper transactions. It might be shorter, for example. So, make sure you enter the account information included from your online banking or investing enrollment package, not your regular account information.

5️⃣ Review the **Account Information** and click **Next**.

6️⃣ Double-check the information one last time, and then click **Done**.

7️⃣ Review the Service Agreement Information that appears, and click **OK**.

Working with the Online Center

You use Quicken's Online Center to connect to the Internet and download information into (or send information from) any Quicken account set up for online access. Periodically, you need to go to the Online Center window and **download** information to use to update your account. For example, you might want to download your bank account information monthly, transfer transactions to the register, as needed, and then reconcile the account. The steps shown here illustrate how to update online banking information.

Task 3: Downloading Account Information

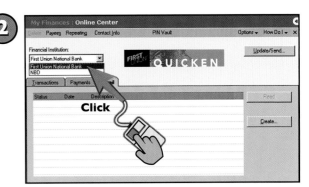

1 Choose **Banking**, **Online Banking** for a bank account or **Investing**, **Online Investing** for an investment account.

2 Open the **Financial Institution** drop-down list and select the name of the institution from which to download information.

3 Click **Update/Send**.

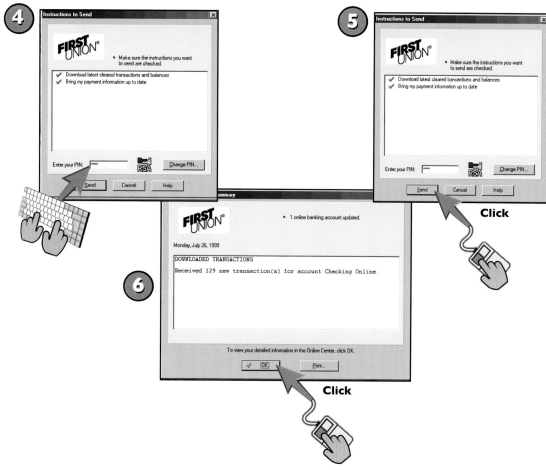

Changing Your PIN

The first time you follow this process, skip step 4, and then you'll be prompted to choose a new **PIN** after step 5. Enter the old and new **PIN** numbers in the appropriate text boxes and click **OK** to continue. In the future, you can click the **Change PIN** button in the Instructions to Send window to change the **PIN** again (for example, if someone finds out what your old **PIN** is and you need to send a new one).

✓ **Disconnect**
If your Internet connection doesn't hang up automatically after the update, double-click the connection icon in the system tray and click **Disconnect**.

✓ **Moving On**
After the download completes, leave the Online Center window open and continue to Task 4 to transfer more information to the account register.

④ In the Instructions to Send window, type your PIN in the **Enter Your PIN** text box. If prompted to change your PIN, click the button at the right.

⑤ Click **Send**.

⑥ When the bank displays a message telling you how many transactions it downloaded, click **OK**.

Task 4: Matching Downloaded Transactions with the Register

Comparing Transactions

After you download transactions, the Transactions tab of the Online Center window lists the received transactions. A **Compare to Register** button also appears on that tab. When you tell Quicken to compare transactions, it identifies downloaded transactions that match transactions you've already entered in the register for the account you access online. It also indicates when a transaction is new, so you can choose whether or not to *accept* that transaction—that is, add it to the register.

✅ **Status Column**
The Status column at far left in the list of downloaded transactions tells you whether Quicken thinks a transaction is a Match or is New.

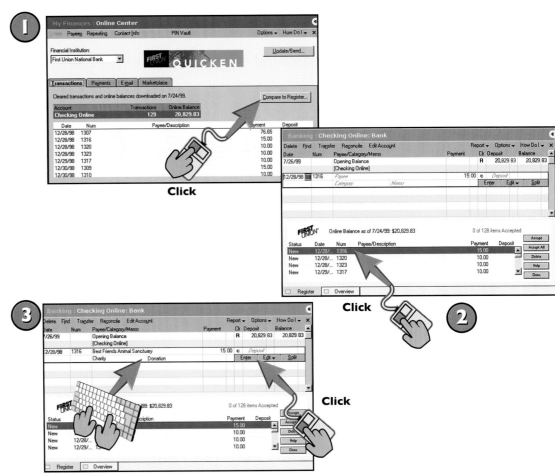

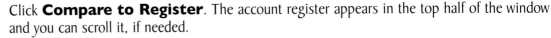

① Click **Compare to Register**. The account register appears in the top half of the window and you can scroll it, if needed.

② For each transaction labeled New, click it in the download list (bottom of window) to create a matching register transaction.

③ Enter missing transaction information (for example, a Category) and then click the **Enter** button below the transaction to accept it.

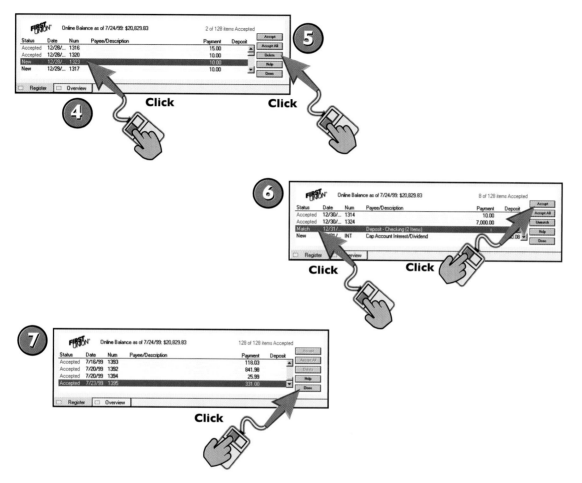

Counting It Down

Note that Quicken counts down the number of accepted transactions above the list of downloaded transactions. Before you finish, make sure you've accepted all of the items; if not, you'll have to manually mark them when you reconcile the online account, as described in the next task. When you've finished accepting and editing downloaded transactions, Quicken returns you to the Online Center window. You can then click that window's Close (X) button to close it.

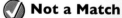 **Not a Match**
If one of the matched transactions isn't really a match, click the transaction and click **Unmatch**. If Quicken can't then match the transaction, it marks it as new, so you can click it and edit the transaction in the register at the top.

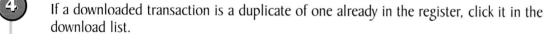

4 If a downloaded transaction is a duplicate of one already in the register, click it in the download list.

5 Click **Delete**.

6 Click each transaction labeled Match and then click **Accept**.

7 Click **Done**.

Task 5: Reconciling the Online Account

Starting the Reconciliation Process

You've already seen how to reconcile a bank account earlier in this book. However, downloading and accepting information streamlines the reconciliation by accomplishing part of the reconciliation work for you. After you finish accepting downloaded transactions, as just described in Task 4, follow the steps here to reconcile those downloaded transactions and print a reconciliation report.

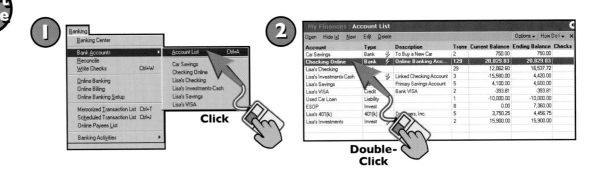

Click

Double-Click

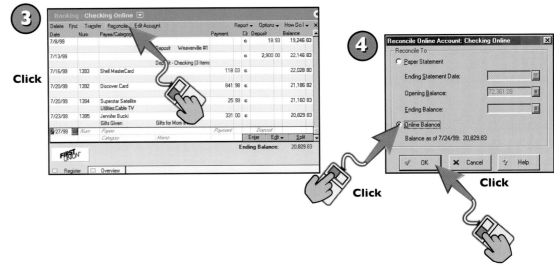

Click

Click

Click

✔️ **C for Clr?**

Notice that the accepted, downloaded transactions have a **c** in the Clr column of the account register. This means that the transaction has been marked as cleared, but that you haven't yet reconciled the account.

1 Choose **Banking**, **Bank Accounts**, **Account List (Ctrl+A)**.

2 Double-click the account you want to open (a lightning bolt in the Type column indicates an online account).

3 Click **Reconcile** on the Register window toolbar.

4 To reconcile, using the already downloaded information, click **Online Balance** and then click **OK**.

Next Step

Understanding Online Reconciliation

Because this reconciliation process only considers downloaded transactions you've accepted and therefore cleared, the Difference shown in the Reconcile Bank Statement window should always be 0.00, unless you've made some type of mistake. If you need help working in the Reconcile Bank Statement window to correct problems, refer to Part 3, Tasks 2–5.

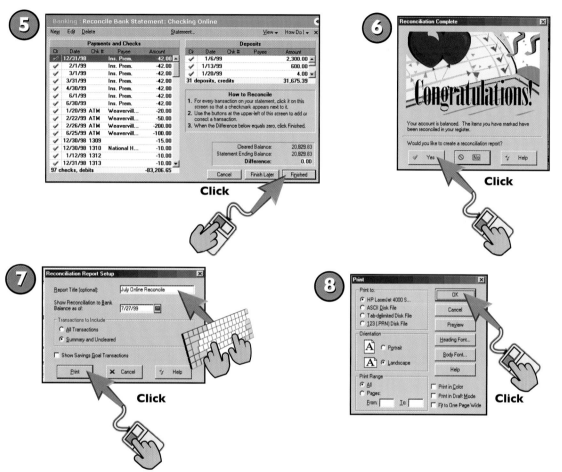

5 Verify that the reconciliation difference is **0.00** and then click **Finished**.

6 Click **Yes** to create the reconciliation report.

7 Enter a **Report Title**, make other report choices, and click **Print**.

8 Click **OK** to print.

Task 6: Entering Payee Information for Online Payments

Setting Up Payees

If your banking institution enables you to pay bills online and you enabled your account for online bill payment (refer to Task 1), you can send payments for your bills without mailing anything. You enter the payment information in Quicken, transmit the payment, and the bank makes the payment for you. The first step in the process is to enter information about each payee. You have to enter your account number and the name, address, and phone number for each payee, so have that information at hand.

✓ Your Institution

If Quicken prompts you to connect to the Internet to update bank information after step 1, do so. Then, if needed, select your online bank from the Financial Institution drop-down list in the Online Center window.

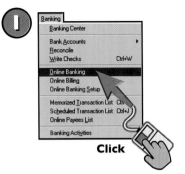

Click

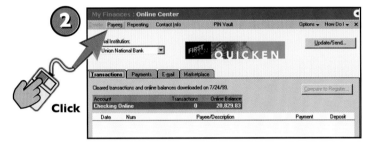

Click

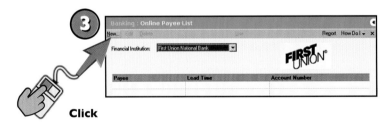

Click

1 Choose **Banking**, **Online Banking**.

2 Click **Payees** on the Online Financial Services Center toolbar.

3 Click **New** on the Online Payee List toolbar.

Next Step

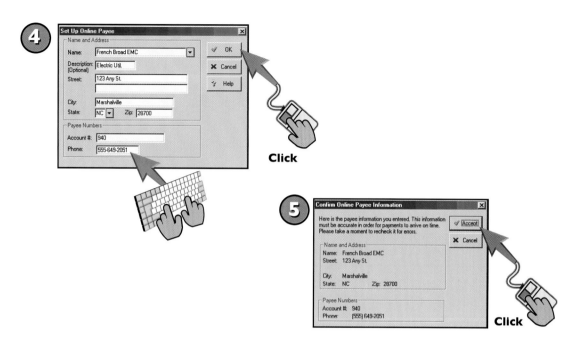

Looking at Lead Time

Notice that Quicken specifies a default lead time for new payees. This lead time refers to how long it takes your financial institution to actually send a payment to your payee. The lead time tells you how long (at the least) before the bill's due date you need to create the payment and send it via Quicken. I suggest giving yourself the due date plus two or three days' cushion time when deciding when to enter online bill payments, as described in Task 7.

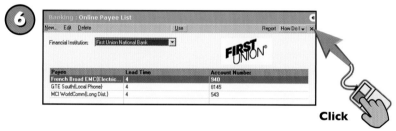

④ Enter all of the information needed to set up the new payee, and then click **OK**.

⑤ Verify the Payee Information and click **Accept**.

⑥ Repeat steps 3–6 as needed to enter other payees. Then click the **Close (X)** button to close the Online Payee List window.

✅ Being CheckFree?
If your financial institution doesn't offer online bill paying, you can sign up for the CheckFree online bill-paying service. See online Help to learn more about signing up for and setting up this service.

Specifying the (Bill) Payment Information

After you have your payees specified in Quicken, enter and send online bill payments from the Online Center window (choose **Banking, Online Banking**). For each bill you receive during the month, you enter a payment and then transmit the payment to your financial institution. The financial institution sends the payment to the payee, using a method the payee can handle (electronic funds transfer or otherwise).

✓ **Delivery Date**
Based on the lead time for the payee you select, Quicken calculates a delivery date for you after step 2.

✓ **More Payments**
You can repeat steps 2–4 to enter additional payments before moving on to step 5.

Task 7: Entering and Sending an Online Payment

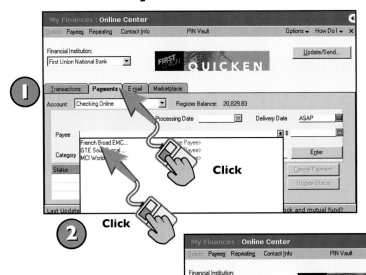

Click the **Payments** tab in the Online Center window.

Click the drop-down list arrow beside the **Payee** line, and click a payee.

Enter the payment amount, category, and memo.

Click **Enter**.

Next Step

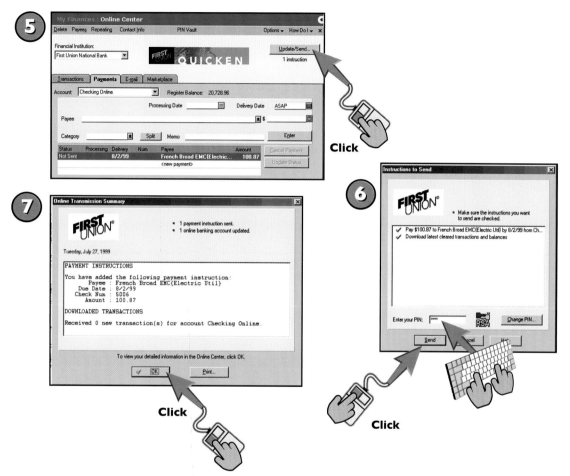

Sending the Payment

After you enter the payment, you transmit it to your bank. Depending on how the bank will pay the payee, it might assign a check number to the payment. If the bank does assign a check number, it picks a number that won't conflict with checks you've written recently from your paper register or Quicken. For each payment you transmit, Quicken enters a corresponding transaction in the account register. Online payments have a lightning bolt in the **Num** field to make them easy to spot.

5 Click **Update/Send**. If you see a confirmation window, click **Send** to continue.

6 Enter your PIN and click to clear the check mark beside any online action you don't need to execute; then click **Send**.

7 Click **OK** after reading the Online Transmission Summary window information.

✓ Printing It
You can print the information about the sent payment from the Online Transmission Summary window. To do so, click the **Print** button there and then click **OK**.

PART

Other Quicken Deluxe 2000 Extras

So far, this book has focused on key areas you need to master to work in Quicken Deluxe 2000. This part covers additional—and sometimes vital—skills you need to round out the knowledge you've built so far. It illustrates how to work with Quicken files and the data in them, how to use two additional tax features, how to research finance topics online, how to organize your records, and how to adjust Quicken features to suit your preference.

Tasks

Task 1: Creating and Opening Another Account File

Adding Another File to Separate Information

If you and your spouse have investments that predate your relationship, you might want to keep those investments in separate Quicken files and use a third file to track your joint financial information. This task shows you how to create a new Quicken file and how to open a particular file.

✓ **Taking a Backup**
Back up the current Quicken data file before you create or open another file. Part 1, Task 22 reviews the steps for backing up.

✓ **Adding an Account**
When you create a new Quicken file, Quicken immediately (after step 4) displays the Create New Account dialog box so you can add an account into the new file. Create the type of account you'd like, as described in various earlier tasks.

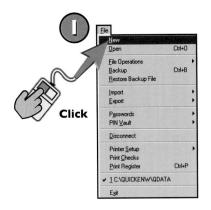

Click

Click

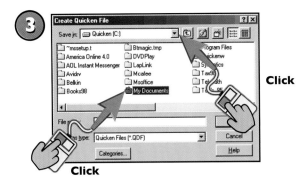

Click

Click

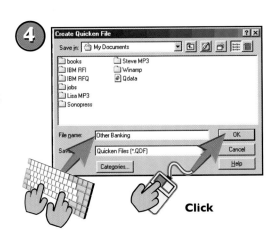

Click

Click

1. Choose **File**, **New**.

2. In the Creating New File window, leave **New Quicken File** selected and click **OK**.

3. If you want to choose a different drive or disk for the new file, use the **Save In** drop-down list and double-click a folder.

4. Enter a name in the **File Name** text box, and click **OK**. Then work through the new account setup as you learned in Part 1.

Next Step

Click

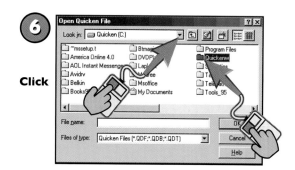

Click

**Double-
Click**

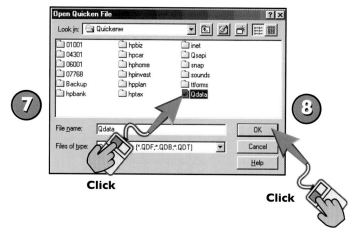

Click

Click

Saving Prior Year Data

When you choose **File, File Operations, Year-End Copy,** Quicken presents two choices: **Archive** or **Start New Year.** Archive copies all of your old transactions, also leaving them intact in the current file. Start New Year moves all of the old transactions into a new file so you can start entering transactions for the new year. Start a new year only if you won't want reports about the prior year's data. In either case, you have to specify a filename for the new file that will hold the old transactions.

(5) To open another Quicken file, choose **File, Open (Ctrl+O)**.

(6) If needed, use the **Look In** drop-down list to choose the disk holding the file to open, and then double-click a folder.

(7) In the Open Quicken File window, click the file you want to open.

(8) Click **OK**.

 Fast Transfer
You can use the import and export features in Quicken to transfer information from an older Quicken file into a new file. See Tasks 2 and 3 to learn more.

Task 2: Exporting Quicken Information

Transferring Account Information to a QIF File

You can export certain types of Quicken information, including account transactions, memorized transactions, and categories you've set up. Quicken stores the exported information into a file with the QIF (Quicken interchange format) extension. After you've exported the information, you can import it into another Quicken file, as described in Task 3. Start the process with the data file that holds the information to export open in Quicken.

⚠️ **WARNING**

If you use the **Browse** button to select an existing QIF file to which to export the data, Quicken overwrites the contents of that file with the newly exported information—be sure to enter a new filename, instead.

Start Here

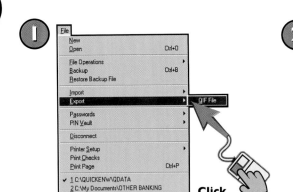

Click

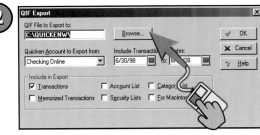

Click

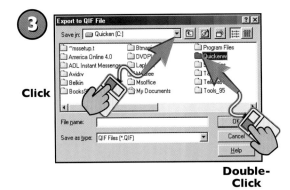

Click

Double-Click

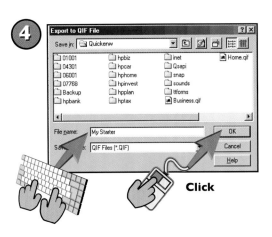

Click

(1) Choose **File**, **Export**, **QIF File**.

(2) If you want to change the folder or drive, click **Browse**.

(3) If you clicked Browse in step 2, use the **Save In** drop-down list to choose a disk to hold the new file. Double-click a folder.

(4) Enter a name in the **File Name** text box and click **OK**.

Next Step

Understanding Quicken's QIF Files

When you create a new Quicken data (.QDF) file, you can import one of your exported QIF files into the data file to set up categories in the data file. At that point, however, you'll need to delete any unwanted transactions and accounts.

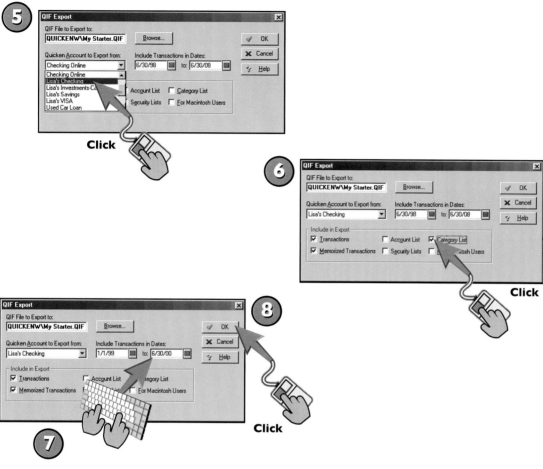

Click

Click

Click

5. From the **Quicken Account to Export From** drop-down list, select the account that holds the information you want to export.

6. Under **Include in Export**, click to select each item to export.

7. If you're exporting transactions, adjust the **Include Transactions in Dates** entries as needed.

8. Click **OK**.

Task 3: Importing Information

Transferring Account Information from a QIF File

After you export information to a QIF file, you can then import that information into any Quicken file. For example, if you and your spouse track certain investment information in separate Quicken files but you later want to combine the information in one account, you can export the transactions from one account and import them into the other. Before you start the export/import process, open the data file into which you'd like to import information.

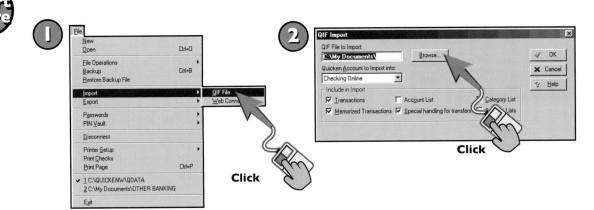

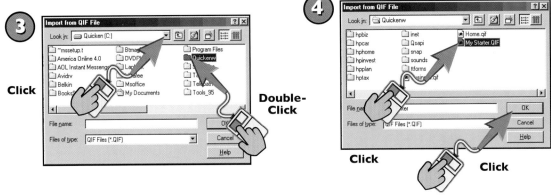

Click

✓ **Checking for Duplicates**
Because Quicken appends imported transactions, you need to check for duplicates.

① Choose **File**, **Import**, **QIF File**.

② If you need to change the drive or folder, click **Browse**.

③ If you clicked Browse in step 2, use the **Save In** drop-down list to choose a disk to hold the new file. Next, double-click a folder.

④ Click a file in the list and click **OK**.

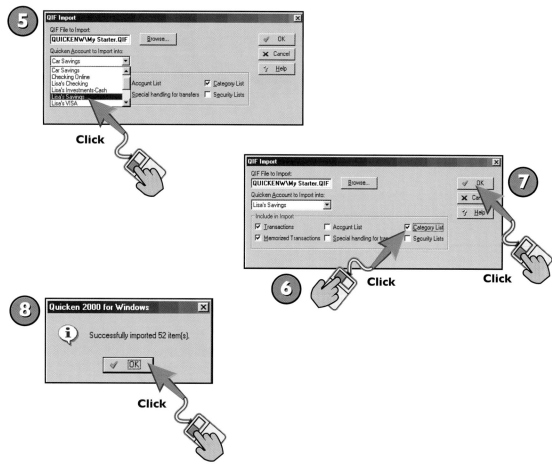

Understanding How Quicken Imports

Quicken **appends** (adds) anything you import to the information already in the file. For example, if the QIF file you import holds five memorized transactions and the account into which you imported already holds two memorized transactions, the account will hold seven after the import.

✓ **Giving It to All**
If you select **<All Accounts>** from the **Quicken Account to Import Into** drop-down list of the QIF Import dialog box, Quicken copies the imported information to all of the accounts in the currently opened Quicken data file.

✓ **Info from Turbo Tax**
To import tax information from Turbo Tax into Quicken, choose **Taxes, Tax Center,** and then click the **Import Tax Data** link to start the process.

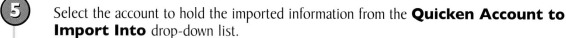

5️⃣ Select the account to hold the imported information from the **Quicken Account to Import Into** drop-down list.

6️⃣ Click to select each item to import under **Include in Import**.

7️⃣ Click **OK**.

8️⃣ Click **OK** when Quicken tells you it has successfully imported items.

Task 4: Using Quicken Information with TurboTax

Transferring Tax Information

Using Quicken, you spend less time working on financial matters but improve accuracy and reporting. For example, you can track information about taxable income and deductible expenses by assigning tax-related categories to transactions (see Part 5, Task 4). At the end of the year, you can import the Quicken information about tax-related income and expenses directly into the TurboTax program (also published by Intuit). TurboTax can calculate your taxes based on the Quicken information. You have to buy and install TurboTax before you start these overview steps.

✓ **Right Version**
The illustrations in this Task show the TurboTax version for Tax Year 1998 (the version available during writing).

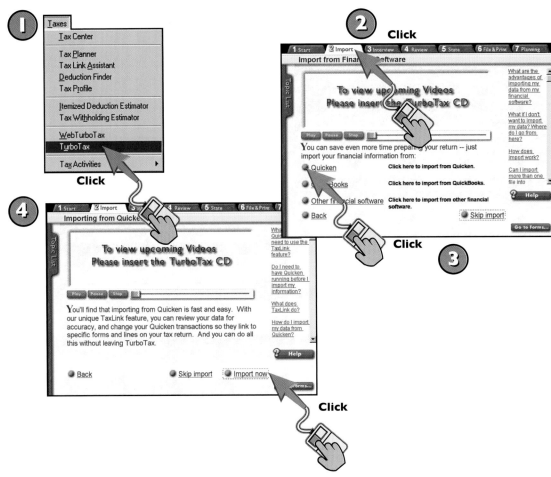

① With the file that holds the tax data open in Quicken, choose **Taxes**, **Turbo Tax** (from Quicken's menu).

② If prompted to register Turbo Tax, do so, and then click the **2 Import** tab.

③ On the Import tab, click the **Quicken** choice.

④ Click the **Import Now** choice.

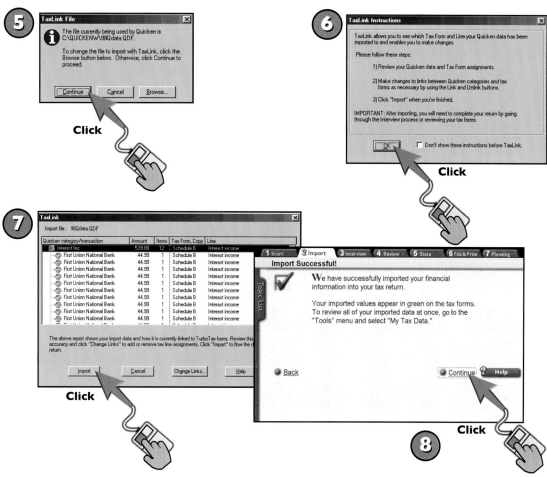

Verifying Information

Quicken and TurboTax, like all other programs, produce results that are only as accurate as the information you enter. If you make a mistake while entering data, your tax information won't be accurate. Always be sure to compare amounts calculated by Quicken or TurboTax with tax reporting forms such as W-2s, 1099s, and so on. If any amounts differ wildly, check your Quicken transactions for the year, make any needed corrections, and reimport the data into TurboTax. You remain responsible for ensuring the accuracy of your tax reporting.

✓ **Good Bargain**
TurboTax costs $50 or so, depending on which version you buy and whether you receive any rebates. The latest version becomes available around January.

---

5 Click **Continue**.

6 Review the TaxLink Instructions and then click **OK**.

7 Click **Import** to transfer the transaction information into TurboTax.

8 Click **Continue** and then finish with your tax preparation.

Task 5: Finding Out More on the Web

Using Quicken.com and Other Web Help

The tax laws change often, and other factors that influence your finances change almost daily. Quicken's makers therefore offer Internet Web sites where you can find information about current financial points of interest or help with the Quicken program. This Task shows you how to get to pertinent sites. In Quicken, you *browse* or review Web pages right within the Quicken window.

✓ Hyperlinks

Web pages use *hyperlinks* (sometimes referred to as *links*). A hyperlink consists of specially formatted text or some type of graphics button. When you click a hyperlink, a Web page covering the linked topic appears. If you point to a hyperlink, a yellow pop-up description box usually appears.

Start Here

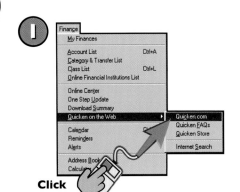

Click

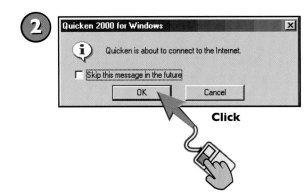

Click

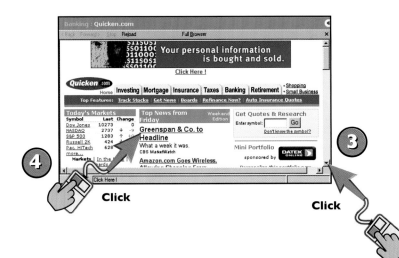

Click **Click**

1. Choose **Finance**, **Quicken on the Web**, **Quicken.com**.

2. If prompted, click **OK** to connect to the Internet.

3. Click to scroll the Web page as needed.

4. Click a hyperlink to display the linked page.

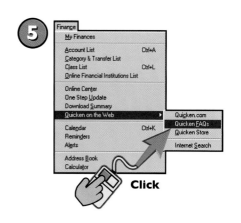

Click

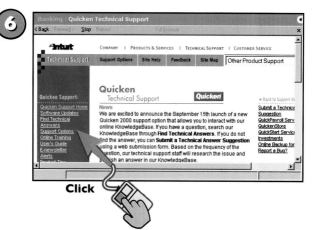

Click

Switching Between Quicken Pages

While you're online, you can simply choose a command from the **Finance, Quicken on the Web** submenu to jump directly to another Quicken-related page. You don't have to disconnect from and reconnect to the Internet first. After you do disconnect from the Internet, however, click the **Close (X)** button to close the browser window.

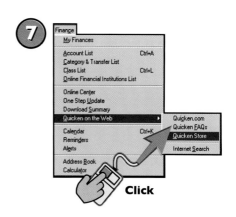

Click

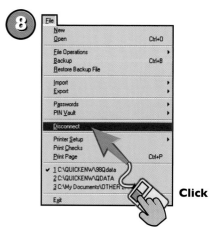

Click

5 Choose **Finance, Quicken on the Web, Quicken FAQs** (frequently asked questions).

6 Browse and use the information for working with Quicken.

7 Choose **Finance, Quicken on the Web, Quicken Store**.

8 After you review any needed information, choose **File, Disconnect**. Click **Yes** to hang up your Internet connection.

Back and Forth
You can click the **Back** and **Forward** buttons on the browser window toolbar to display a page you've previously viewed.

End Task

Task 6: Getting Online Investment Information

Using Quicken Investment Research

Quicken provides you the key tools you need to track your investment results. However, you generally won't experience positive results unless you make a good investment decision in the first place—and doing so requires research. You have to review statistics and background information to understand what type of investment you're buying and to understand the risk level and potential for returns. You can find investment research through Quicken, using its Investment Research Web site.

✅ **Mutual Fund Search**
If you scroll down farther on the initial Investment Research window, you'll see text boxes for entering a mutual fund ticker symbol. Use one of them and the accompanying button to search for information about a mutual fund.

Start Here

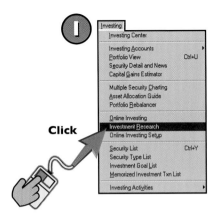

Click

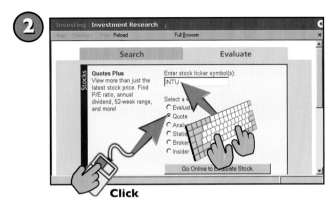

Click

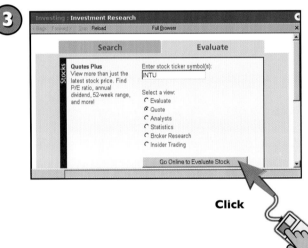

Click

1 Choose **Investing**, **Investment Research**.

2 Enter the applicable stock ticker symbol and click the option button that describes the type of research you want.

3 Click **Go Online to Evaluate Stock**.

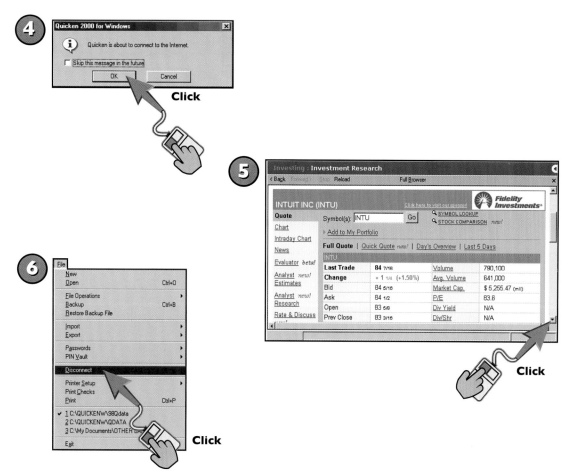

Exploring the Information Offered

The various pages of the Quicken Investment Research Web site offers links along the left side. These links lead to even more detailed information about investments, as well as helpful tools to help you identify an investment to purchase. For example, the first Investment Research page includes a Rate & Discuss link, which you can click to access message boards about the selected stock and others. Bottom line: You'll find a lot to explore here, so exploit the Quicken Investment Research site to the fullest extent.

④ If prompted, click **OK** to connect to the Internet.

⑤ Scroll down to review your search results.

⑥ When finished with the Quicken Investment Research site, choose **File**, **Disconnect**. Click **Yes** to hang up your Internet connection.

Task 7: Using the Asset Allocation Guide

Setting Up Your Asset Allocation

Your asset allocation refers to how much of your money you've got invested in particular types of investments. The idea is to have different types of investments to reduce your overall portfolio risk. In Quicken, you can set up a target asset allocation and compare your portfolio to it. Start by opening the Quicken file that holds the investment account(s) to work with.

✓ The Best Advice...
Be sure to consult a professional financial planner if you want detailed guidance about asset allocation.

✓ More Guidance
Quicken's Asset Allocation guide provides even more help than this task describes, such as model portfolios with suggested asset allocations. Follow links throughout the guide to learn more.

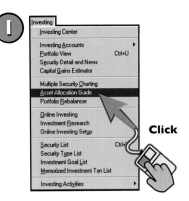

Click

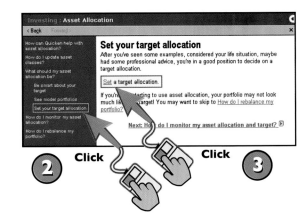

Click **Click**

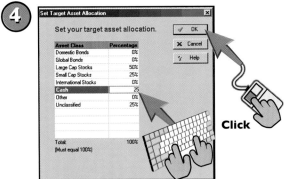

Click

① Choose **Investing**, **Asset Allocation Guide**.

② Click **Set Your Target Allocation** at the left side of the Asset Allocation window.

③ Click **Set**.

④ Enter applicable percentages and click **OK**.

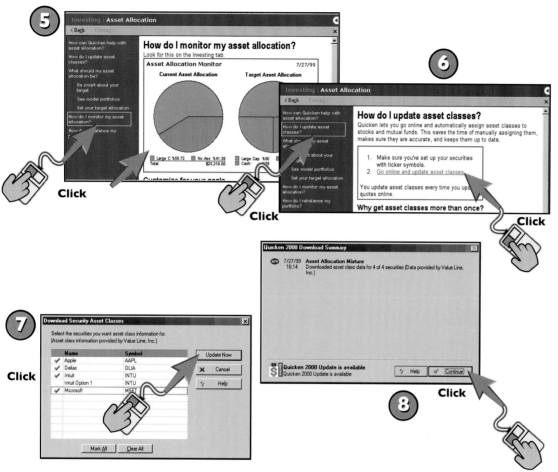

Downloading Asset Class Information

When you set up different types of investments (securities) in Task 2 of Part 4, you specified an asset class defining whether the security is a large cap stock, small cap stock, or other type of investment. In steps 6–8, you tell Quicken to go online, verify the specified asset classes, and update that information for your portfolio. View your portfolio again as described in step 5 to see the updates.

✅ **Quick Take**
Click the **Investing QuickTab**, then scroll down to the **Asset Allocation Monitor** section to see your current and target asset allocations.

✅ **Portfolio View Update**
You also can update asset classes from the **Portfolio View** window. Choose **Get Asset Classes** on the **Update** menu on the toolbar, then proceed with step 7.

5 Click **How Do I Monitor My Asset Allocation?** and review the comparison of your target and actual portfolios.

6 Click **How Do I Update Asset Classes?**, and then click **Go Online and Update Asset Classes**.

7 Click to place a check beside each security to update, then click **Update Now**.

8 Click **Continue** after the asset class information downloads. Choose **File**, **Disconnect** and click **Yes** to close your Internet connection.

End Task

Task 8: Using the Stock Screener

Finding Stocks to Buy

While the asset allocation help you learned about in the last task gives you overall guidance about what types of investments to buy, finding those investments is another matter. Quicken enables you to go online and find stocks that match particular criteria you specify, so that you can get more information and decide whether or not to purchase a particular stock.

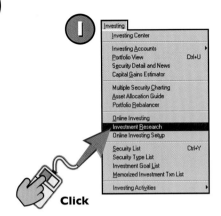

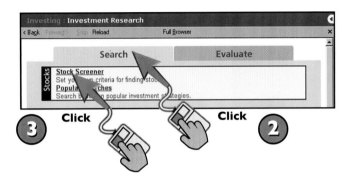

✅ Screening Other Investments

The Investment Research window also includes links you can click to screen for mutual funds and bonds.

① Choose **Investing, Investment Research**.

② Click the **Search** tab.

③ Click **Stock Screener**.

④ Click **OK** to connect to the Internet.

Next Step ▶

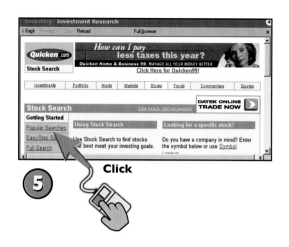

Click

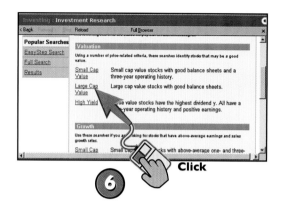

Click

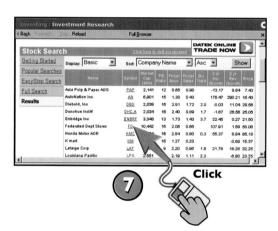

Click

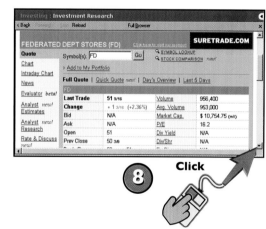

Click

Browsing Stock Information

Once you've displayed a particular stock (step 7), the left side of the Web page displays a series of links to detailed information about the selected stock. Click a link to view more information, and click the **Back** button on the toolbar to return to the prior page of information. You also can keep clicking **Back** until you see the Stock Search page, and begin a new stock screen.

✅ **Other Searches**

In the Stock Search Web page shown in step 5, you can choose the **EasyStep Search** choice to screen stocks by answering a list of questions. Click **Full Search** to screen by specifying 33 different criteria.

⑤ On the Stock Search page, click the **Popular Searches** link.

⑥ Scroll down, and click the link to the **Valuation or Growth** category that best describes the kind of stock you want.

⑦ Scroll down, and click the ticker symbol for a stock you want to investigate. Scroll down to view information about it.

⑧ Click links to stock information as needed, and disconnect from the Internet when finished.

End Task

Getting an Online Quote

The rates for comparable insurance policies offered by different companies can vary dramatically. You could spend hours providing information to agents to gather a number of quotes, or you can go to the InsureMarket Web site (via the Quicken.com Insurance site) to get quotes for a term life or auto insurance policy. If you fill out a brief questionnaire and specify your coverage needs, InsureMarket returns quotes from the likes of Prudential, MetLife, Zurich, John Hancock, and State Farm. After you find a policy that suits your needs, you can apply for it online.

WARNING

Don't purchase your insurance policy based on the rate quote alone. Make sure you read every detail of each policy to know what you're buying.

Task 9: Shopping for Insurance with Quicken InsureMarket

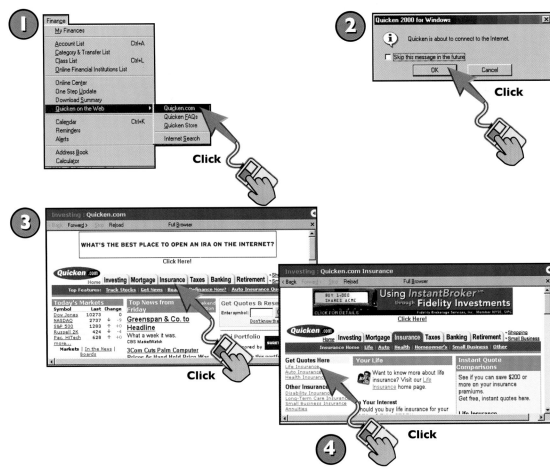

Start Here

Click

Click

Click

Click

1 Choose **Finance**, **Quicken on the Web**, **Quicken.com**.

2 Click **OK** to connect to the Internet, and click **Connect** if prompted.

3 Click the **Insurance** tab.

4 Under **Get Quotes Here**, click the link to the type of insurance for which you want a quote, such as **Life Insurance**.

Next Step

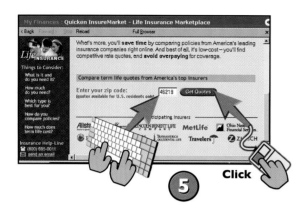

Click ⑤

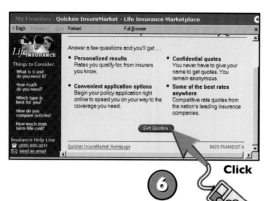

Click ⑥

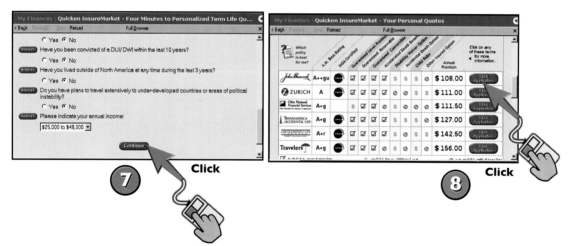

Click ⑦

Click ⑧

Exploring Other Coverage

As for Quicken's Investment Research site, the Quicken.com Insurance site offers more than can be shown in a brief lesson. Your choice in step 4 determines what type of information follows. You can come back to either insurance site as often as you need, learning more about insurance, identifying when you might need to change coverage due to life changes, or even applying for and buying a new policy.

✔ I'm Lost

The quoting process varies a bit depending on the type of insurance you're buying, so follow the links. Also, online quotes may not be available depending on where you live. In such an instance, InsureMarket displays a link you can click to get in touch with local insurance agents for a quote.

⑤ Scroll down if needed, enter your zip code, and click **Get Quotes**.

⑥ Scroll down and click **Get Quotes** again.

⑦ Respond to each screen of questions, clicking **Continue** after each page.

⑧ Scroll down to display rate quotes, and click **Start Application** to apply online for any quoted policy.

End Task

Task 10: Shopping for a Mortgage with QuickenMortgage

Shopping Online for a Mortgage

For many, buying a home is the single most expensive purchase we'll ever make. Coupled with the stress of finding the right home, you have to find the best mortgage to pay for it. Use the QuickenMortgage Web site (accessed via Quicken.com) to facilitate this process without having to talk to multiple loan officers. QuickenMortgage can help you pre-qualify for a mortgage, compare rates from dozens of participating lenders, and even apply online. This task illustrates how to get started.

⚠ WARNING

When you arrive at the point of applying for a mortgage, a fee is involved. Sometimes you can get an in-person lender to waive a loan application fee, but if you find a loan online that's more competitive, you could easily save more than the application fee.

Start Here

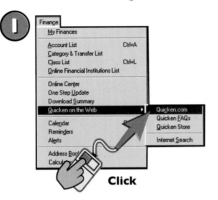

Click

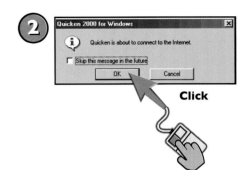

Click

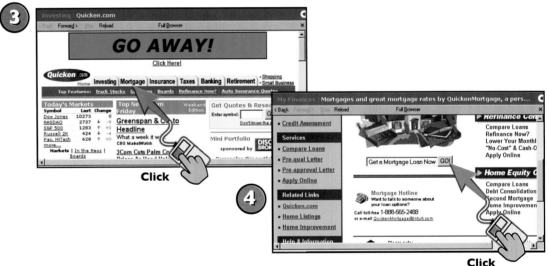

Click

Click

1 Choose **Finance**, **Quicken on the Web**, **Quicken.com**.

2 Click **OK** to connect to the Internet, and click **Connect** if prompted.

3 Click the **Mortgage** tab.

4 Review the introductory information, scroll down, and click **Go!**.

Next Step

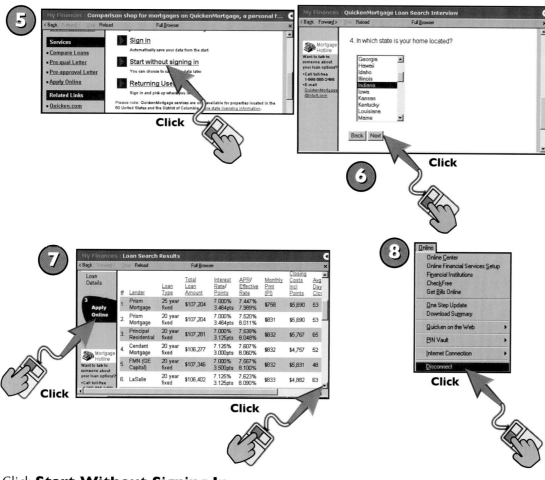

Finding Other Mortgage Information

The QuickenMortgage Web site also offers links not explored here. For example, in step 4 you can click links that take you to tools for seeing if you can afford a more expensive house. Feel free to do any of that kind of legwork on the QuickenMortgage site before you begin the process described in this task.

✓ **Signing In**
Click the **Save Your Data** button on any screen to enter a username and password, and save the information you enter on the QuickenMortgage site. The site then stores information you enter so you can resume work at a later time without re-entering everything. Click the **Sign-In** link (see the illustration for step 5) the next time you access the site.

5 Click **Start Without Signing In**.

6 Following all of the onscreen prompts, enter the needed information and click **Next**.

7 Scroll down to view the loans that match the criteria you specified. Click **Apply Online** if you want to complete an online application.

8 When you finish working with mortgage information, click **Online**, **Disconnect**, and click **Yes** if prompted.

Keeping Important Records

Quicken's Emergency Records Organizer enables you to capture a variety of information that normally might be scattered in files, a safe deposit box, an address book, and so on. Emergency Records Organizer tracks information about people to contact in case of emergency, medical history information, locations of legal documents (such as a will or birth certificate), details about property you own, and so on. Start by entering a *record* for each piece of information, as follows.

✅ Privacy Alert

The records you enter might contain very sensitive or private information. To keep it secure, create a new Quicken data file, enter the Emergency Records Organizer information, and assign a password to the Quicken file.

Task 11: Using Emergency Records Organizer

Start Here

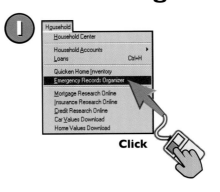

Click

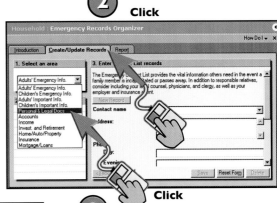

Click

Click

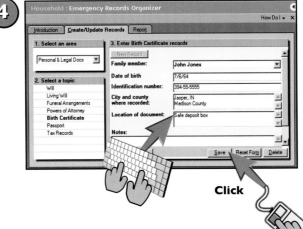

Click

① Choose **Household**, **Emergency Records Organizer**.

② Click the **Create/Update Records** tab.

③ Make a choice from the **Select an Area** drop-down list.

④ Click a **Select a Topic** choice, enter record information, and click **Save**.

Next Step

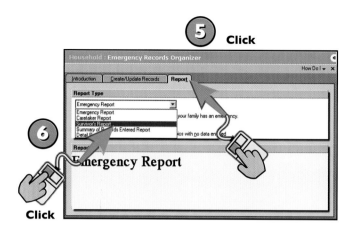

Click ⑤

Click ⑥ ... Emergency Report

Click

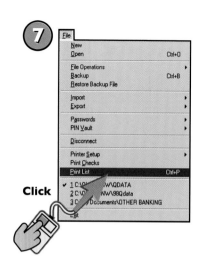

⑦

Click

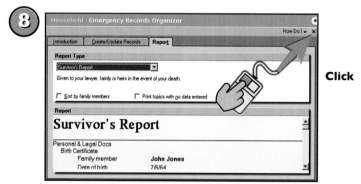

⑧

Click

Printing a Report

After you've entered all of your records into the Emergency Records Organizer, the payoff is that you can print a report that provides information you need. Depending on the type of report you select, Quicken automatically plucks out applicable records and includes them in the report. For example, a Survivor's Report displays records about your legal documents and property to aid in resolving your affairs. An Emergency Report contains emergency contact information and medical records. You can print a report from the Emergency Records Organizer anytime you need one.

 Updating
Update your emergency information at least twice a year or whenever you make a change such as opening a new bank account.

⑤ After repeating steps 3 and 4 to add all records, click the **Report** tab.

⑥ Select a report type. The report appears at the bottom of the tab.

⑦ Choose **File**, **Print List** to print the report.

⑧ Click the **Close** (**X**) button to close the Emergency Records Organizer window.

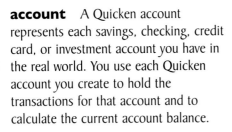

account A Quicken account represents each savings, checking, credit card, or investment account you have in the real world. You use each Quicken account you create to hold the transactions for that account and to calculate the current account balance.

Account List An alphabetized list of accounts in a Quicken data file. Select the account to work with from the Account List.

Account Overview When you click the Overview tab in the account register, Quicken displays Account Overview information, including basic account information, recent account statistics, and graphs. You can update account information in the Account Overview or click links to perform operations pertaining to the account.

alert A special warning or message you set up to appear in the Reminders window. For example, you can set up Quicken to alert you when a checking account balance falls below a particular amount, such as the minimum required by your bank.

Asset Allocation Guide A Quicken Deluxe feature that enables you to divide your investment dollars among different types of investments, to better position your portfolio to meet your financial goals.

back up Creating an extra copy of your Quicken data file on a particular date, to preserve your data in case the original file becomes damaged. *See also restore*.

balance When you've cleared all transactions while reconciling the account and the difference between the Cleared Balance and the Statement Ending Balance is 0.00, the account is *balanced*.

Billminder A Quicken feature that appears when you start Windows to alert you of an upcoming scheduled transaction.

browse Move from Web page to Web page by using Web browser software.

browser See *Web browser*.

budget An expense and income plan you create in Quicken. Quicken can then compare your budget to actual expenses and income you enter, showing the difference left for savings and other purposes.

category A label used in Quicken to identify an income or expense, so Quicken can report on how you spend your money and where it comes from. *See also subcategory*.

Category & Transfer List A window in Quicken where you can edit and add new categories for tracking transaction amounts.

checking account A Quicken account that corresponds to your real-world checking account. You can enter payments (bills) in the checking account and use Quicken to print checks to pay those bills.

cleared balance The total amount of cleared transactions.

cleared transaction A transaction you check off while reconciling your account, because the transaction has been executed by your bank or financial institution. You can mark a transaction as cleared when your account statement (from the bank or financial institution) shows the transaction. *See also reconcile*.

data file See *Quicken data file*.

deposit A transaction for money added into a Quicken account.

download The transfer of a file from one computer to another, often using a modem and telephone line.

EasyAnswer Report A type of Quicken report that focuses on a very narrow range of information, such as how much you're saving or the total payments (amounts) assigned to a particular expense category.

ending balance   The current account balance that Quicken calculates by adding and subtracting transaction amounts from the opening balance you specified when you created the account. *See also statement ending balance.*

field   In a register program, one piece of information you enter for a transaction, such as the payee.

Financial Activity Centers Areas in Quicken that group features for particular aspects of financial management, including Banking, Investing, Household, Taxes, Planning, and Reports and Graphs.

find   Search for and display one or more transactions that match criteria settings you specify.

font   The particular design of the characters in a report. Each font has a name, such as Arial or Times New Roman. You select the font by name to apply it to a selection.

graph   A visual representation of the entries in one or more Quicken accounts.

group   Classifies similar categories and subcategories, such as those that represent discretionary expenses.

hyperlinks   Specially formatted text, buttons, or graphics you click on a Web page to display (jump to) a different Web page.

insertion point   The flashing vertical mark that indicates where typed text appears in a field or dialog box.

Internet   The worldwide network of computers that stores and transfers information.

Internet account   Dial-up Internet access you purchase from an Internet service provider. When you obtain an account, you receive an account name and password you use to connect and log on via your modem. After you connect to your account (your Internet connection), you can use a browser to work on the Web, use your email, and so on.

Internet Connection Wizard (ICW)   A feature in Windows that leads you through the process of creating a Dial-Up Networking connection so your modem can dial up and connect to your Internet connection.

Life Event Planner   Quicken tools found in the Planning Financial Activity Center that enable you to determine how much you need to deposit over a particular period of time to accumulate a particular amount of money to reach a goal such as a set amount for retirement. Some financial calculators also enable you to calculate potential loan or refinancing amounts.

links   *See hyperlinks.*

memorized report   A customized report you've saved for reuse.

memorized transaction   A saved transaction you can reuse or copy into your register and update as needed. QuickFill can automatically save transaction information for each new Payee or Paid By entry you make in an account. You can also use the Memorized Transaction List to add and work with memorized transactions.

Memorized Transaction List The list that stores your memorized transactions.

modem   A device that enables your computer to communicate with another computer via telephone lines. Newer types of modems enable your computer

to communicate via special higher-speed phone lines, cable television connections, or even satellite.

My Finances Center This initial window displayed by Quicken includes handy lists and reminders: the Accounts List, Alerts and Reminders, Scheduled Transactions, Securities Watch List, Monthly Income and Expenses, and Credit Card Analysis.

new transaction line The next available line in a register. Enter the next new transaction in this line.

online banking Setting up Quicken to transfer information from your bank or financial institution directly into a Quicken account.

opening balance The balance you enter when you create a new account, based on the most recent statement balance for the real-world account tracked by the Quicken account.

payee The recipient of the funds from a check or withdrawal transaction or the source that paid you the funds for a deposit transaction.

postdate Entering a future date for a check transaction, so you can print or pay the check at a later date.

Quicken data file A file that holds Quicken accounts. Although a

Quicken file can hold multiple accounts, you might want to create a separate data file for each person using Quicken, to keep information separate.

QuickEntry 2000 A companion program for Quicken that displays only an account register and a few basic commands. You can enter transactions in QuickEntry instead of Quicken when you don't need or want to see all of the features in the full Quicken program.

QuickFill A feature that memorizes a transaction for each new payee (creating a memorized transaction) and enables you to quickly fill in that transaction information when you begin typing the payee's name in a new transaction.

QuickTabs By default, Quicken displays a QuickTab at the right for the My Finances Center and each of the six Financial Activity Centers. As you work in each center, Quicken adds another QuickTab for each activity you open or account you create. Click a QuickTab to select its window, making that window the current or active window.

reconcile Comparing a Quicken account with the paper account statement from your bank or financial institution. Reconciling involves clearing and adjusting Quicken transactions to make them match the statement so

ending balances for both the Quicken account and the statement are identical.

recurring transaction See *scheduled transaction*.

register An account register holds the entries for your account. The register for bank accounts (for example, checking and savings accounts) looks very similar to your paper checkbook register.

reminders A feature that reminds you to use an upcoming scheduled transaction. Reminders appear when you start Quicken. You control how far in advance a reminder appears.

Reminders List The list of dates on which you've specified that Quicken should remind you of an upcoming scheduled transaction. *See also reminders*.

report Specially summarized or grouped information in Quicken. You can print the report after displaying it.

restore Using a backup copy of your Quicken data file to replace the current version if it becomes damaged.

scheduled transaction A check or payment transaction or deposit (such as a pay deposit) that happens at regular intervals. Quicken reminds you of each scheduled transaction and enters the transaction information for you, if you want.

Scheduled Transaction List
The list of scheduled transactions you've entered in Quicken.

scroll   Viewing a different area in a file or list. Usually accomplished by clicking a scrollbar on the side or bottom of the window.

split   Assigning more than one category or subcategory to a transaction to reflect accurately the purpose of the expenditure or the source of the income. You specify the portion of the transaction that falls into each category or subcategory.

Start menu   The menu that appears when you click the Start button at the left end of the Windows taskbar. The Start menu enables you to access the startup command for Quicken Deluxe 99.

statement ending balance
The ending balance from your paper bank statement, to which you compare your Quicken transactions when you reconcile your account.

Stock Screener   An online tool that you can use to research and select stocks.

stock split   An entry you make in an investment account to adjust for a real-world stock split, in which the issuing company grants one or more additional investment shares for each share you currently own.

subcategory   A subdivision of a Quicken Deluxe category, used to identify an expense or income transaction more precisely. *See also category*.

tax estimate   A calculated estimate of your Federal taxes, based on approximate values you enter at the time of calculation or on Quicken data you've entered previously.

Tax Planner   A Quicken feature you use to generate a tax estimate.

tax-related category   A category you identify as tracking either a taxable income or expense. Quicken uses the information from tax-related categories to generate tax reports and estimates.

toolbar   The toolbar appears along the top of the active window in Quicken, well below the menu bar for the Quicken application itself.

transaction   A bill (check), deposit, transfer, withdrawal, or ATM action you record in a Quicken account.

transaction group   A list of transactions you collect under a group name and schedule in the Scheduled Transaction List. You can select a transaction group from either the Scheduled Transaction List or the Quicken Reminders window to enter all

of that group's transactions in the register simultaneously.

transfer   A transaction that withdraws money from one account and deposits it into another account.

Uniform Resource Locator (URL)   The address for a particular file on the Internet, such as the address for a particular Web page. Also called an *Internet address* or *Web address*.

void   Marking a transaction as no longer valid, but leaving it in the register to leave the check number intact so Quicken correctly numbers subsequent checks.

Web (World Wide Web)   A subset of computers on the Internet storing information you can display graphically by using a Web browser.

Web address   *See Uniform Resource Locator*.

Web browser   A program that enables your computer to display graphic information downloaded via modem from the World Wide Web.

window   Holds a particular type of information within Quicken; for example, the Memorized Transaction List window.

Index

commands

graphs

P

W-Z